PROPERTY FOR THE NEXT GENERATION

VICKI WUSCHE

Liability disclaimer

The information contained in this book has been gathered and collated from the experiences of the author. Every effort has been made to make sure the details are accurate.

However, they are experiences and by that nature, and the fact that they have been gathered into a book, means that they will be in the past as you read this.

It is vital that you take this information and check its relevancy to your personal situation and to the marketplace right now. We have been through ten of the most unprecedented years in the economy, all rulebooks have been torn up and no one knows what the future holds. It is the lessons of the present that carry us forward.

In uncertain times it is easy to panic. Some become paralysed by fear and indecision, others rush forward in an effort to get rich quick before it's too late – whatever that means!

Please take this information, learn from the mistakes, benefit from the successes and, above all, carve your own future in the shape you desire. Identify your resources, define your goals, recognise your personal needs and then focus on creating and achieving your personal investment plan to secure your family through these uncertain times. Sadly this won't be the last time in your life time that we face global uncertainty.

WHAT PEOPLE ARE SAYING ABOUT
PROPERTY FOR THE NEXT GENERATION

66

This book's greatest strength is that it takes conventional financial wisdom and re-examines it before suggesting an alternative (more prosperous) path. Relying on fund managers to provide a paltry 3% return on a pension fund will have serious repercussions for people and Vicki argues in a logical, practical way about why people shouldn't be fatalistic about their financial future and how, with an open mind, one can change this (regardless of age). An excellent read.

— JAMES

66

This book is a straight-forward read that explains simply why the younger generation are at high risk of poverty in their later years if they do not make provision for themselves to protect the future. Vicki Wusche, a successful business woman, has secured her own future with property investment and associated businesses and clearly wants to help others achieve the same. Well worth the read and if you haven't read Vicki's other books to which this one is a supplement,

I highly recommend that you look up "Using Other People's Money: How to invest in property" (4th edition) and "Make More Money from Property: From Investor thinking to a Business Mindset" (2nd edition)

— JUDITH

"

'Unlike many property books, Vicki doesn't just talk about strategies. She talks more about realising what I want from my life and how property can get me there. I like Vicki's philosophy.

— NICK

"

This is a thought-provoking book. Bringing together to key issues that both we and our children will face. The rising cost of property means it is harder for our children to get on the property ladder, combined with political uncertainties and the damage they bring to the finance markets. If you have children then read this book – one of Vicki's key messages that you don't have to live where you own or own where you live has helped me rethink our family strategy.

— MARK

66

These are challenging times and you would be right to think twice about property investment or any large financial decision. Vicki's second edition of this book is a perfect reminder not to panic and to think clearly about how you can help your children and grandchildren navigate this maze of bad news, mis-information and chaos. Read it and then give to your kids to read, then buy a copy for your parents!

— JEFF

66

'I finished Using Other People's Money: How to invest in property this morning [after reading Make More Money from Property: From investor thinking to a business mindset]. I really found both of your books a fantastic read with plenty of gold nuggets to take away. So thank you for the great value you've added to my life, looking forward to reading your next book!'

— LUKE

66

"A timely book that encourages good old home economics with action taking, with the end goal of securing prosperous futures for ourselves and our children."

— LORRAINE

ALSO BY
VICKI WUSCHE

Using Other People's Money: How to invest in property. Fourth Edition. SRA Books, 2016. ISBN: 978-1-909116-65-8

Make More Money from Property: From investor thinking to a business mindset. Second Edition SRA Books, 2017. ISBN: 978-1-909116-96-2

The Wealthy Retirement Plan: A revolutionary guide to living the rest of your life in style. IAM 2019, ISBN: 978-1-912615-85-8. Released January 2019

The New Estate: Insights from the 22ⁿᵈ Century. Wusche Associates Limited. ASIN: B00WR2R6HE

GRATITUDE
FOR LESSONS LEARNT
& TEACHERS ALONG THE WAY

I have travelled a long and bumpy road from redundancy in 2006 to this place of wealth, friendship and love. There have been many lessons, realisations and insights along the way.

I am so grateful to all my family – to my darling Bob, my daughters Kimberley and Charlie, my new granddaughter Amelia, her insightful father Lee, and all my supportive friends – without whom the journey would have been longer, less fun and much harder.

My business team is now filled with too many to name individually, but you know who you are. You know how much I appreciate you and that you are valued.

I would like to thank everyone who has worked with me, either through my investment business, as a mentee, client or a business partner. You help me to push my boundaries and gain new insights, which enables me to keep creating new and future-proof sustainable business models.

Remember everything in life is either a gift for a lesson already learnt, or a lesson to help you gain a new gift. Count your blessing and be grateful for your lessons. I look forward to meeting you at some point in our near futures.

CONTENTS

CHAPTER 5

Teach your 22-year-old
to buy their own house

FOREWORD

BY VICKI WUSCHE
MOTHER AND GRANDMOTHER OF
THE NEXT GENERATION

I t may seem odd to write my own foreword, but I want to write to you as a parent and grandparent (although I am far too young!). Like you, I'm concerned about the uncertain times ahead of us and the impact that could have on my family's future.

Uncertainty is nothing new. Generations before of us, and those yet to come, have faced all forms of uncertainty from micro-family focused changes created through the natural cycle of life and death, marriage and divorce, employment and redundancy to the macro-global uncertainties of war and financial chaos.

I feel that we are at a global pivot point starting with the Arab Spring of 2010, through the Trump election and Brexit vote of 2016 to a series of political shifts across Europe and the world as a series of elections demonstrated a change of ideology. It is too early to say whether this ideological change will result in a better world or not.

What can be seen, is the impact on global finances as the shifts to more uncertain times follows close behind a deep and prolonged global financial crisis.

How can we as individuals, parents, employees and business owners make any difference on a global stage? Well, some of you will (and have) through the casting of votes in elections. Some of you will through the ideas and changes that you ripple out from your family to your community and beyond.

In April 2015, I wrote my fourth book entitled, *The New Estates; Insights from the 22nd century.* It was a story about a world 85 years in the future. I imagined an ideal life and set out what would have to change in the preceding years for my dream world to become a reality. I saw a future where we all took responsibility; first for ourselves and then for our families and then widened that out to our communities and ultimately our country. Apathy and entitlement no longer existed. Rights came with responsibilities. I did away with bankers' bonuses and benefit payments. Everyone had enough, and everyone contributed.

We can demonstrate financial resilience and prevent ourselves from becoming a burden to the younger generation by taking complete responsibility for our own financial security and financial future. All it requires is good planning, and for that planning to start now.

What has this got to do with Property for the Next Generation?

When facing uncertainty, the one thing we must do is ensure our family is secure. Because of my background, I believe the first point of danger for any family is finance. The impact of job losses and redundancy can devastate a family, not only through the loss of income and the ensuing stress, but through the ultimate damage it does to the family structure and the life of the children within in that unit. I experienced this even though I knew my own redundancy was coming.

I am passionate both about property and the foundation that a decent home provides. At my lowest point, I was stuck in a violent marriage that I felt I had no escape from. I didn't have enough finance behind me to escape. We had lived for years on benefits during the latter part of my marriage. As I left the marriage with nothing, I adopted a process of writing down on a notepad every penny I spent, including ten pence to make a phone call (please tell me you remember phone boxes – I am not that old!).

My parents' home provided an interim base for me to regroup (with my two young daughters), and then thankfully the council enabled me to become a social housing tenant. Without those stepping stones, which I know so many people do not now have access to, I would not be who I am and where I am now.

Having lived through this process, my daughters know the value of financial resilience. We should all teach our children about finance, and show them that money is a tool which can make them financially secure for life IF invested well. I know that could seem a challenge. It does not need to become a source of arguments and badgering in the house. It must be discussed along with the changes we are experiencing and challenges we are facing. It must be demonstrated by you in your everyday behaviour. My children have seen me go from living in social housing, to building first my own property portfolio to ensure my family's futures are secure. This is very important to me. I have helped many people start and grow their own property portfolios that provide the same financial security to their families.

We need to recognise that property has a significant role to play in the stability of our personal financial futures and the life of our communities. All wealthy investors have significant property portfolios. So should you, if you want to secure your financial future.

The media stories of a housing market crisis frequently fall back on blaming landlords as an easy, and to some, palatable excuse. The tax changes by the Conservative government in early 2016, indicated to me that they want to see the end of the private rental sector (PRS). They want to stop ordinary people like you and me from investing in property for our pensions, for our children and as a business which offers decent homes to decent people. They would rather see all property bought up by large corporations and private equity firms. Had this been the case in 1992, when I moved in with my parents, my life would have taken a much darker path.

My fear is that large organisations are focused solely on profit. Don't get me wrong; I run my property portfolio to make a profit, but not at the expense of my clients, my tenants. I think the future of the PRS and the UK as a whole will be seriously damaged if this comes to pass. It also closes the door on personal financial responsibility, community responsibility, caring and The New Estate, the new concept of how we could live I described in my book of the same name.

In uncertain times, people will always need somewhere to live. We can provide those decent homes for decent people, while generating a fair and reasonable profit to support our own families. That additional income from investments can then become the financial cushion that protects you now, and generations to come, against the fear of redundancy and financial collapse.

INTRODUCTION

WHO ARE YOU AND WHY ARE YOU READING THIS BOOK?

As you've chosen this book, you are likely to have some or all of the following:

- A worry about what will happen in the coming years

- A concern about how the tax changes will impact on the property market

- A constant eye on your finances

- A worry about your financial future

- Or maybe an existing property portfolio which is not performing as you expected or is in danger due to tax changes

You may also have:

- A great job with a substantial income or a successful business which you have been running for a number of years

- You own home with a relatively low mortgage

- A family that you love, but that costs you a fortune
- No time and more stress than you would like
- School fees to pay
- University fees to fund
- Activities and hobbies for both you and your children that you would love to engage in but lack the time or the money
- Savings or bonuses in the bank doing nothing
- A pension which won't give you the retirement you want

Above all, you know there must be a better and easier way.

WHO AM I AND WHAT GIVES ME THE RIGHT TO WRITE THIS BOOK?

In summary:

- I work with clients to identify the lifestyle that they want to live and the under-utilised resources that could, if properly leveraged, make this dream a reality. On a day to day basis, my business teaches clients how to run their own successful businesses, in a variety of markets, including property, and helps bespoke clients invest in cashflowing property.

- This is the third book of five that I have written, and it is in its second edition. I excel at sharing what I have learnt about wealth and money, as I established my businesses and applied the theories of property investment.

- I have taken financial responsibility for my family.

- I have two daughters, one studying medicine at university in Slovakia and the other in her own home. She bought this with no cash from me – only my advice and support.

- Bob is my life partner; dive buddy and best friend and we spend our time enjoying life.

- I am busy, often travelling around the country speaking, but it never feels like work – I love what I do.

- I don't have a pension – I have a property portfolio. I am effectively retired from traditional working life.

- I don't have 'savings' – I have constant cashflow.

- I don't have to work – so, effectively, I am retired and doing what I love. I have a well-funded Non-Traditional Retirement. I choose to contribute my knowledge and experience for the benefit of others.

- I watch the markets and the economy with amazement and curiosity, not stress or worry.

Above all, I have found a better way. I won't say it was easy, but I am now taking responsibility for my financial future and it feels much better, and the accountant tells me it is better.

❙ HOW CAN YOU KNOW WHAT YOU DON'T KNOW?

Like you, I went to school. Then, at the age of 28, after my divorce, I went to university. I achieved first-class honours and then a Master's degree. I obtained teaching qualifications and became a university lecturer. I learnt my way off benefits and into work.

Yet, no one EVER discussed the implications of using a credit card, interest payments or how to buy a house. No one talked about how money really worked or how I could get it to work for me!

No one ever explained how the beliefs of my parents might be influencing the choices I was making in my life. Or that those beliefs would become a challenge, even hindrance, to my success given the dramatic rate of change happening in the financial world, business, technology, global and European economies.

I constantly heard and still hear ridiculous statements about the way life should be... founded on myth, half-truths, marketing spin and gossip.

Myths like:

> "WE SPEND MORE MONEY NOW TO BUY
> OR RENT OUR FIRST HOME THAN OUR
> PARENTS DID."

I agree, but we earn a lot more too. Yes, in some areas of the country there is a disconnect between family income and property prices – but that is solvable.

> "YOUNG PEOPLE HAVE TO LIVE AT
> HOME FOR LONGER."

Is that such a problem? A decade or so ago, we coined the phrase 'Empty Nesters' for parents who missed their offspring. Why can't we live together without stigma? Why can't our children move away and then come home again? Why can't we be more flexible, open and connected?

> "YOUNG PEOPLE CAN'T AFFORD TO BUY
> THEIR FIRST HOME UNTIL THEY ARE
> 35-40 YEARS OLD."

That is exactly why parents need to plan now. I believe it also suits some young people, who have changed career or just finished university and have travel plans, to remain mortgage free. It is cheaper to move between rented accommodations than to sell and rebuy property.

"BUY TO LET INVESTORS ARE STEALING THE HOMES THAT FIRST-TIME BUYERS WANT TO BUY."

Rubbish. Speak to an estate agent and they will tell you that young people like my daughter would never consider buying a stinky mess in need of a new kitchen and bathroom. They want to buy a property that is already refurbished. This is because the refurbishment is included in the price and the mortgage and not a direct additional cost to their pocket.

I want to take a tired or derelict property and renovate it to a decent standard, adding value along the way. It was the government that stimulated the property market and increased prices from 2014 onwards with the Help to Buy Scheme and by allowing those over 55 years old to access money early from their pensions! Not Landlords!

"THE RENTAL MARKET IS UNSAFE AND UNSTABLE – TRUE."

I would love to offer two-year rental contracts to my decent tenants, but current legislation and lenders prohibit this. It is only in recent months the government has started to discuss this much-needed change. I want my tenants to think of my property as their home. I want them to stay for the long-term.

When it comes to safety and decent standards

– I agree a small percentage of landlords fall below decent standards but then so do a small percentage tenants. The market lacks a sense of responsibility that comes with the right to quietly enjoy a property.

For everyone's sake, let's create landlord and tenant registers; then we can build the trust that is so lacking in the market. When you do wrong, it will appear on your record – it's that simple. It will be public and then tenants will be able to choose their landlords, based on feedback and a star rating. Landlords will also be able to choose their tenants based on a good score as well – like reviewing a restaurant or a good movie.

There is a contradiction in government policy and a lack of joined-up thinking. One department sells off existing property under the right-to-buy, selling properties in prime locations at a discount. Then another department is forced to buy property on the open market at full market value to replace the stock!

Therein lies the problem!

In 2007, as a single parent who was out of work through redundancy, I started to learn about money and how it really worked, as I realised that I needed to be able to make informed decisions. I refused to continue living my life by the unconscious rules and filters that my parents, teachers, peers, press and even the government had imposed upon me. I needed facts, not media-manipulated gossip and speculation.

I did not realise, even as a teacher working

within the education system, that school was failing our children – the next generation. School was failing to equip my own daughters for life in a complex environment that's driven by global dynamics.

Luckily, I was unconsciously sharing my understanding and experience with them. My experiences, as tough as some of them were, have actually helped me to teach my children how to function in this debt-driven volatile economy.

Who is teaching your children? Who is explaining to them:

- How money works
- About good debt versus bad debt
- Why the rich get richer
- How working long hours in a high paid job won't make you rich or happy
- Why some families seem to be able to buy property for their children and yet other families have 'children' in their 30s, even 40s still living at home
- How, as a single parent, I could help my daughter buy her own home?
- Why the whole property market is in chaos and society is suffering as a result
- The more I had to experience and cope with, the more I realised it was like someone had

been keeping a secret that I hadn't even known existed. Now that I knew it existed, my next challenge was to discover exactly what other people knew that I did not.

- Who knew the critical secrets that would help me change my life?

- What exactly did they know?

- What was going to be important in my life and in the life of my family going forward?

The next section will share more details of the rocky patches of my life, and what I had to recognise and learn to get my family financially secure. It will explain in detail the insights and the triggers that generated the lessons I have learnt, in order to show you that every challenge provides a lesson that we need to learn. Within this learning is the door to the next phase of your life, a way out of the box that you may feel you trapped in.

Learn from my lessons and experience. Short-cut your learning journey please. I wish someone had shared these insights with me right from the start. Also recognise how I turned each challenge into a lesson or insight. This ability to adapt and learn will be vital as we face these uncertain times. The next decade is likely to bring us political change, global restructuring and technology that could make the financial crisis feel like a light breeze.

MY STORY AND HOW I LEARNT THE LESSONS THAT SCHOOL WILL NEVER TEACH YOU

I am sharing my story so that you can understand the real value in this book and why I am so passionate about sharing this knowledge. My story is relevant in that it will help you to understand why I feel so strongly about empowering people with true financial understanding, the amount of experience I have, and why I was driven to write this book. It will also add the context – the richness and the drama. If you read carefully between the lines, you will see how our world is changing irrevocably as I write, just as I had to face challenges and uncertainty, so will we all. It's not just Brexit and political instability, but also the increasing globalisation and interconnectedness – with business and money knowing no borders nor boundaries other than those imposed by negotiations – and how that is continuing to impact, both implicitly and unconsciously, on our everyday lives.

The simpler life of a child

Without dwelling on the past for too long, I was a happy and perhaps privileged child by some people's standards. I used the word 'privileged' because I don't remember wanting for anything or seeing my parents struggle. As an adult, I can now reflect on how hard my parents worked: my father as a tailor, who ultimately got his own shop, and my mother, who first worked as a shop owner and then in the bar and restaurant trade to fit her hours around school times. We had a foreign holiday every year – we travelled across Europe by car (a little Fiat 500) to Italy to see my father's sister and wider family.

I lived in a world (not too long ago) where I was happy to get an orange and my Girl Guide's Book wrapped up from Father Christmas. The branded, labelled, technological world of the X-Box and iPad had not impacted on my need for material things. Life was easier, simpler and, dare I say it, cheaper – and I am really not that old!

I also don't ever remember hearing phrases like 'money doesn't grow on trees' or 'money is the root of all evil'. I had no feelings attached to money – it really was not on my radar.

While I loved playing with the tills in my parents' shops, and I worked with them from around the age of 12 years, I was not overtly entrepreneurial – I didn't create business ideas and sell things to friends. I got my first 'official' Saturday job at 16 and enjoyed it. I saved up and bought an expensive camera and then, as soon as I could, bought my first car – they were functional items rather than luxuries. I wanted to go to Portsmouth to study underwater photography (like Jacques Cousteau). Money was a tool. Money was accessible.

The downside of my 'privileged' life was that my family never discussed or managed money in front of me, so I had no concept of budgeting or saving. As an adult, I realise that they must have managed their money very carefully because we were not rich in the financial sense, but we lived well. I can actually remember my mother buying that extra tin of Spam®, ham or corned beef (yuck) each week in the shopping in the weeks running up to our holiday so that she could take it with us. Despite Italy being renowned for its amazing food, we would cater for ourselves, with mum's rations, rather than going out to eat. What my dad could conjure up with a tin of corn beef would make a cordon blue chef cry! I also have a vague recollection of my father having a budget for each day of the holiday. We never discussed money.

Money? Not a clue

When I got married and my husband 'managed the money', because that's what men seemed to do, I was surprised and deeply embarrassed when our home nearly got repossessed because he had not been paying the mortgage. I had been completely unaware of this. How could I have let it happen? Worse, I started to see a pattern...

Before we married, he hadn't paid the rent on the flat we briefly shared and we were forced to move. Our first home was sold just before the bailiffs came.

Our second home was sold the day before it was repossessed, while I was lying in a hospital bed having our first daughter, as the stress of impending repossession had brought on early labour. I am not abdicating responsibility. Back then, I had a full and happy life and was unaware of the importance of taking responsibility – financial or otherwise.

What was I thinking? I honestly don't know! Money was just not on my radar. As you can imagine, that all changed – it had to change!

Hard lessons about money

The first set of lessons came as the marriage broke up in violence and I fled to my parents with two baby daughters. I slept in their back room for a month or so while I tried to sort my life out – emotionally, financially and literally. I was lucky, there was still the council system of housing people in need of support, and I was shipped off to Brent to live in social housing. While it was just forty minutes' drive from my parents' home, it may as well have been a million miles away when you have no car and two babies and only public transport as an option.

I now know that the owner of the house that became our home for nearly three years had given their property over to the housing association on a lease. We were finally moved back to Uxbridge, as we were ultimately that council's responsibility, into yet another social housing property. This time our home was owned by a collection of investors leasing it to the council for five years. When the lease was up, the council gave me an ultimatum: I either bought the house or would be moved again. My children were settled in school and we were close to my parents. I simply could not bare to move again.

Luckily by 2001, Bob and I had by then been together for over two years and made the massive, and somewhat forced decision, to buy the house together. Actually, we still live in that same house today. I could never have committed to that massive purchase on my own, and I am so fortunate that Bob is such a wonderful partner and that the decision worked well for the whole family.

Between 1991 and 1999, life settled down to a routine of financial budgeting and money management on a scale that I had never experienced. I imagine that some families have been doing this kind of budgeting for the last ten years, as the impact of the recession started to hit households.

I literally counted every penny. I worked five jobs while studying for my first degree and then 'just' two jobs during my Master's. During term-time, I taught in front of students for 30 hours a week, which meant another 60 hours of preparation and marking had to be squeezed in. My daughters became very disciplined and went to bed early (by today's standards) so that I could study for my Master's degree or mark students' work.

I saved for holidays and managed a trip to the Maldives, where I finally qualified as a scuba diver – my absolute passion. I then saved again and took the girls, who were aged seven and nine, to South Africa on the road trip of a lifetime. For six weeks, we travelled from Capetown to Durban and places in between. The experience of visiting the KwaZulu Natal region in the east of South Africa had a profound effect on all three of us as we learnt what it really meant to be poor. The family units – devoid of males because they had to leave to find work in the city – were governed by the great-grandmother. They survived in circular thatched huts, gathering firewood, rubbish to recycle and lived in hand-me-down clothes. However you may feel right now, you are still one of the richest people in the world because you can afford to buy this book.

Making money work for me – the start

I learnt how to work credit cards to my benefit, I will go into detail about credit cards and what you need to know later in the book. I enhanced my financial skills with credit cards so that by the time 0% credit cards became available, we were able to buy our home from the council and 'offset' my mortgage interest by borrowing money on credit cards and holding it in a linked savings account.

I actually borrowed money for nothing and used it to offset the cost of my mortgage at 5–6% saving over £7,000 per year. Now the credit card companies charge an admin fee, but if you are clever, you can still borrow money for 3-4% over 18 months to two years and so reduce the cost of borrowing to 1.5-2%. This could still be cheaper than your mortgage.

However, I was still an employee with no idea about how money really worked. I was just stumbling onto strategies and using common sense to make them work. I recognised how I could borrow money for free, while other people were borrowing the cheap money and using it to buy material possessions, increasing their actual debt.

I honestly think that my failed marriage and time as a single mother gave me the skills to manage money that have proved invaluable throughout the rest of my life and the lives of my children. It is not something that I would recommend – as you read this book you will gain an understanding of all the things that I could not have learnt without the pain and trauma of divorce!

On 9th of September 1999, my life took another turn. I broke my arm while out on a bike ride and was rescued by Bob. We have been together ever since – my own knight in sweaty lycra. This is not really because we were hardcore off-road cyclists covered in mud – but he is still my hero. I now had a partner in my life again, but still no real idea about money, the future or anything.

Over the next seven years, I would move from

being a part-time/contract lecturer, working six or seven contracts at a time, to a job funded by government on an annual basis. This would be a massive change in terms of job security for me, certainly compared to the university. But, still, as a family, we never completely knew what was happening financially for more than six months at a time. Budgeting and being 'careful' with money was still an underlying theme.

Redundancy and a change of direction

Then, in late 2005, I found out that funding for the quango I worked for was to stop and by the summer of 2006, I was made redundant. I had loved all my jobs and particularly loved this period. I had been working with education providers at a strategic level to shape education to meet the needs of local people. I worked with professional refugees as a director of a charity, helping them to requalify, and I sat on the board of directors of another government-funded regeneration project looking at the whole scale regeneration of South Kilburn in West London – this involved working on issues like housing, education, crime and 'young people'.

In late 2006, I had a go at being a consultant, but found I was working for free for all the people who used to work with me when I was funded by the government – that was technically a period of unrecognised unemployment and totally unsustainable! We must have tightened our family budget, changed our habits to account for having less income. I have no real memory of this – money was not really on my radar.

I am sharing this detail so you can see that I am just an ordinary person living an ordinary life. My experiences have taught me lessons that would become so valuable that they enabled me to become successful as a property investor. More importantly, I have created a property portfolio that will provide security for my family at a time when uncertainty, redundancy and financial insecurity dominates the news. I learnt through experience so you can learn these lessons now.

Retraining my mind

In 2007, I discovered personal development and I learnt how the mind worked. How we have a subconscious mind that is designed to protect us, and even a higher or spiritual mind that can inspire us. I welcomed the opportunity to explicitly learn again and soon qualified as a Master NLP practitioner (Neurolinguistic Programming) and hypnotherapist.

More important than the paper-based qualifications, I became a master of my own mind. I started to recognise how the guilt that I felt for the failure of my marriage and its subsequent impact on my daughters was shaping everything I did. I was so focused on helping others – students at university, business and education providers through the Learning Partnership and then the residents of South Kilburn – that I was not paying any attention to the long-term needs of my family, and perhaps not paying attention to their immediate needs either.

Some people I speak to feel uncomfortable with the idea of increasing their personal wealth. That, I am sorry to say, is rubbish. We all need to increase our personal wealth – to become self-sustainable and to stop relying on the government to help because it just can't afford it anymore!

In 2007, I had no savings and actually had nearly £80,000 on credit cards. I also started to recognise that I had no job either. I used my credit cards again to pay for my personal development and support me through the training. While that made my material debt worse, it paid off all my emotional debt and cleared the path for a truly wealthy life.

Somewhere along the way, I read an incredible book by James Redfield called *The Celestine Prophecy*. It told the story of a young man on a journey and how he learnt there were messages and signs all around him – opportunities if you like – and his lesson in life was how to recognise them. That is a key lesson I would love you to learn – there are lessons all around us. Maybe buy a copy of *The Celestine Prophecy* and read it for yourself.

I had read this book years before, but with my new understanding of how my mind worked, the book made a lot more sense. I had looked at property for years. First, as a child, when my grandparents had died and my parents moved house, and then through my own house purchases and near repossessions. I also watched my friends and had been taking it all in, storing it up for later, for when I was ready to process it consciously. And the time was now – I was ready.

The property journey begins

To step back a little, in 2004, after many years of disagreement about the actual investment strategy, my sister and I borrowed money from my parents to invest in a buy-to-let flat in London. We used the services of an experienced investor to buy the flat using a mortgage and then leased it to the council in return for rent. The rent was more than the cost of the mortgage and so we got to keep the profit. After a while, as house prices rose, I remortgaged the flat and bought another, and then repeated the process.

Then the world changed...

In 2007, I was aware that something was happening to the economy. I didn't understand what exactly but knew I needed to pay attention. I started to listen to the news, watch current affairs programmes and have different types of conversations. I learnt that some people thought that the property market was going to crash, that prices would fall, partly because, in economic terms, they could not rise forever.

We all know that was just part of the story. Extraordinary banking practices called 'derivatives' meant that banks could sell 'bad debts' wrapped up in insurance policies to one another for profit. If you are interested in this extreme insanity, then read the three books by Dass, Morris and Rajan that are referenced in the Bibliography.

The world economy started to collapse with the weight of mounting and unpaid debt. The point is that if you lend money to people who cannot repay you, then you don't have a business, you have a liability, and that cannot go on for long.

I made the decision to remortgage the flats we had in London for one last time to pull out our equity, at effectively the height of the market. I didn't consider the impact of interest rate rises and I have to say that we have been extremely lucky.

These properties were such good investments they have managed to remain cashflowing even in the darkest days of the economy and at the height of the interest rates.

Property full time

In 2008, I decided to start investing in buy-to-let properties as a full-time career. The property prices were falling and I understood more about money than I ever had in my life. We even had a small London portfolio to whet our appetite.

As a family partnership, we all chipped £25,000 into a pot. We all got trained and then decided that

I would do all the work as the others preferred the security of employment. In effect, my family became my first sourcing clients. Over the next year, I only managed to complete the purchase of one property and I really struggled. The lessons taught by the property training companies had made it all seem so easy. The reality was much harder.

What none of my property training courses or books explained was how the changes in the economy would impact on anyone investing in property. This was my job; my business and it was under threat. No one predicted banks would suffer so badly and spiral into a period of lending shortages because of their past practices. The money traded on the markets between lenders, and then lent out to us at a profit, would virtually dry up, and interest rates would first rise steeply as inter-lender confidence faltered. Interest rates would then fall to the lowest on record as the government had to intervene to control the risk of spiralling inflation.

Time to get serious

In November 2008, I made the decision that I was either going to be successful or go and work in the local supermarket stacking shelves at night. I set my goals and through my own determination set about buying one or two properties per month on average for myself or clients throughout 2009. By mid-2010, I had enough net rental income (profit) to cover my household expenses so I would never have to have a 'normal' job again.

I published my first book and started the first of my two property businesses. I began to formally find, source, property deals for clients who had cash they wanted to invest in return for more money than they could get from the banks.

In the period between the time I started full-time property investment in late 2008 and the autumn of 2010, I had turned our family portfolio into a cashflowing business.

What does this have to do with the title of this book? Watch what happened next. Bob and my daughters have lived through my 'mind enhancing' last few years, like the saints they are. They listened and adapted as I spouted on about how we needed to take responsibility for our own lives and not blame others. I have shared a distilled version of that understanding with you as I have explained the myths and the facts of life.

They also watched as I bought property after property. Bob visited properties with me and understood the concepts and the numbers involved. In 2009, he started to become more involved in the business – he had to, as he was party to many of the mortgages we now have. My younger daughter, Charlie, came with me on the buying trips and saw the properties we own. After all, in the end, the portfolios will all belong to Charlie and her sister. It's funny that she now works in my business – who would have guessed?

My elder daughter, Kimberley, was not interested. You cannot force your children to see how important this is – you have to be patient with them. This means you should start buying property in your name and then wait for them to ask what you are doing. Occasionally, we had conversations that hinted she wanted me to buy her a house. I made it very clear that that was not how it worked. We invested our money to make a profit, a salary if you like.

Buying more property in the South did not make sense from an investment point of view, especially when I could earn so much more in comparison by buying further north. I will go into the mathematical detail of property models later in the book so you can start to grasp the scale of the opportunity that I am presenting to you.

The journey to help my child buy her own home

In 2010, Kimberley's questions started to change as they became more about the concept of buying a house, what would be needed and what was the process. I explained the stages she would need to go through step by step. In the final section of this book, I have shared those steps with you in an easy-to-understand way that is also easy to put into practice, if you so choose.

In early 2011, Kimberley started to actively look for a house. Again, I shared my knowledge and understanding of the market. I helped her to understand how to narrow and refine the searches. We started to view properties together and I explained what to look for, how to speak to vendors, what questions to ask and how to decide the amount that should be offered for each property.

Within months, Kimberley had chosen the property she wanted and negotiated the purchase offer price. The next step was to fully embrace the mortgaging process. After a delay caused by the vendors, she moved into her first house in November 2011. By 2012, Kimberley was already discussing how she could buy a second property for investment purposes – and so increase her monthly income.

The more recent future in a nutshell

In 2016, within just six months, I bought 14 properties for clients. By spending £849,000 of their £2.2m pot, I generated an average of 15% net return. In the last 8 years, I have bought 65 properties and raised over £5 million in Joint Venture money.

I did this whilst not on holiday scuba diving as my alter-ego (The Property Mermaid) and enjoying every aspect on my Non-Traditional Retirement.

By that I mean I am not retired, nor do I consider myself employed full-time. I choose how to spend my time and work on projects and businesses that excite and interest me – when I want. I still manage my own portfolio, and my sourcing business and training company continue to develop and thrive.

I still provide sound business consultancy to growing businesses and entrepreneurs outside of property, enabling them to really obtain the entrepreneur's dream of more time, more money and more control in their lives. So many of my clients had other businesses that needed reorganising before they could invest in property that this just became a natural extension of what I offer. After all property is just one form of business.

I have continued to write books, five now in total. My fifth book is due for release in January 2019.

We have an amazing life, blessed with a new granddaughter. And so the cycle begins again. Please let this be the start of us helping you. By understanding the part that *Property for the Next Generation* can play, we can create financial security for all our families.

WHAT IS IMPORTANT FOR YOU AND YOUR FAMILY MOVING FORWARD?

This book will explain in plain English how you can help your child invest in property. You will not need to give them £10,000 or even £100,000. Instead, you will share with them your understanding of how both money and the mind work, which I will teach you in this book. In fact, by the time you get to the end of this book, your children might recognise that they don't need to own the home they live in – they just need to own cashflowing properties and use the rent to live anywhere they want.

You could use property to create an income stream to increase your overall family income, or to pay for your children's private or university education. You might plan to invest in property as a retirement vehicle for yourself and your partner or to help your children start their own businesses. What you choose to do will depend on your current circumstances and your future plans. This book will take you through that thought process and help you to shape your ideas into a personal investment plan and a cashflowing property portfolio.

This book will explain everything you need to know in order to teach your children how to manage their finances and invest in property. Everything school failed to teach you – and them! In other words, property and property investment for the next generation. Their success will be yours as you get older and do not have to rely on their generosity because you, as a family, will become collectively wealthier.

WHAT IF YOU DON'T TAKE ACTION NOW?

If you don't take responsibility for your own financial future, then you will face an impoverished retirement with drastic implications for your children and grandchildren. You will leave a burden of debt and commitment as you drag out your remaining retirement years in a care home, draining them of every penny they will not have. To read more about why you need to take action now, read my latest book about Non-Traditional Retirement and why you need a plan.

There are direct implications of your inaction for your children:

- They won't have you to turn to, to understand the power of investing, and managing money
- They won't have a family portfolio supporting their parents (you), so they will have to step in
- The family portfolio will not become a legacy for the grandchildren

But and even more important than this is the practical implication that you will not have taken the steps to help then invest in property now when it is cheaper than it will be in the future. For all the reasons I will explain later, property will only ever go up in price. There might be temporary or localised adjustments over the coming years, but in the long-run it's a simple supply and demand issue – prices will rise. Your children will find it increasingly harder to get on the property ladder because they don't have you to support them (through experience and understanding) and they simply can't afford it.

Notice I don't use the word 'home' in any of my explanations. The property my daughter lives in is her home, of course, but it is also an investment property. I have explained to her that this property has been bought at the best time to invest this generation will ever see.

This is not about emotion; it's about business and wealth creation. Emotion is reserved for the life you live knowing you are financially secure.

▌PROPERTY IS AN INCREDIBLE ASSET

Property is tangible, in demand and controllable. We know there are not enough houses. We also know that, as an island, there are only so many houses that we can ever be built in the UK. People need to live somewhere, and with a growing population, it is clear the demand for property will only increase.

As long as you continue to repay the mortgage debt, you will be able to control the use of any property you own. You will control its potential to generate an additional income.

You can choose who lives there, what rent they pay, whether or not to renovate or split the property into private rooms. As I influence your understanding of market demands and property investment as a business model you will make new and improved choices.

You will become more attuned to the economic environment we live in. Not the version of the economy expressed in *The Sun, The Mirror* or *The Daily Express*, but the shocking reality that we are standing on the edge of a precipice. 2016 saw us all make decisions which will impact on all our families for eternity.

ARE YOU GOING TO TAKE RESPONSIBILITY FOR YOUR FINANCIAL FUTURE AND THAT OF YOUR FAMILY?

You are already someone who realises that things need to change; that the world our children are facing is so dramatically different from our 'simple' lives and that we need to prepare them, not burden or shackle them with our debt. They already have the government's debt to repay! You are already different from the masses who just don't realise we are facing yet another earth-shattering finance storm. You understand that we need to prepare and take action. Why? Because you are reading this book.

The following chapters will explain how you need to think differently about money, property investment and the future of your family. The rich will continue to get richer because they understand this stuff. This book will take you through the seven myths we face and the seven lessons you need to learn and share with your family.

I will explain the explicit strategies, step by step, which you can follow to help your child buy their own house. The caveat is that they need to be over 18 years old to hold a mortgage. If your children are younger, then you can start buying houses for them now while property prices are cheaper than they will be in just a few years. You can get advice on ways to invest for your younger family – or your family as a whole when the time is right. Now consider the principles and open your mind.

PROPERTY
FOR THE NEXT
GENERATION

CHAPTER

1

RECOGNISING YOUR FINANCIAL LANDSCAPE

I f you are busy working, often spending long hours away from your family, and you are happy with that, then maybe there is nothing wrong with the way things are. However, this whole book is written on the assumption that you are working long hours, and you don't feel valued or wealthy. You don't feel relaxed, and you are worried about what the future might hold financially.

To add to your worries, your private pension has dropped significantly in value as the stock market fluctuates. Your bonus accumulates in the building society or as bonds, but it is earning you nothing. The government pension can no longer be relied upon to help. Not only that but the country voted to leave the EU, and you are now unsure about the stability of your job or business.

Your children will expect to leave home and get a home of their own. How will you be able to help? You will still be paying off their school and university fees. They will be paying off their university loans. So even with all this money flowing around your family, you still do not feel rich and don't feel that your family is financially secure.

WHAT ARE YOU REALLY WORRIED ABOUT?

Even as the press share their statistics and poll results, which we now doubt, telling us how difficult it is to buy your property, our worries turn towards the impact of Brexit. Will currency falls impact business and job security? Will the money currently being spent on European contributions really be redistributed to those in need here in our country? When can my family move home, invest in property and stop feeling financially stressed?

I spoke at an event a few years ago, and one member of the audience said it did not seem fair that I should help people to invest in property when others could not afford it. That's like saying I shouldn't throw a drowning person a life ring or tell them how to swim because the others could not hear me!

I hold a belief that 'charity begins at home'. We cannot afford to make excuses or to waste time. We must act now and take responsibility to secure our own family's financial future. Once we are secure, we can help others. In effect, that is what I am doing.

In the end, not everyone will own their own home. That is fine; not everyone owns a business. Some people are employees and are very happy with their choice. Property is the same – some people want to own while others want to rent. I will explain shortly how you won't have to live in a property that you own or own a property in which you live. You will be able to benefit from additional cashflow.

Our opinions are frequently shaped by what the media tells us, but we all need to start deciding what we think for ourselves, based on facts.

London is vastly different from the rest of the country. Here, property prices definitely exceed the normal affordability of most local people. Numerous reports and press investigations show how vast numbers of properties are owned by foreign investors in off-shore tax havens. This will continue until legislation is changed to make London a less desirable place to invest, especially with favourable Euro currency exchange rates.

The mayor's plans to build more affordable homes is not a solution. Reinventing council estates, whether to rent or buy, is missing the point. There are already empty properties in London which can be put to better use.

This is mirrored across the country, from derelict properties in the North to empty office blocks. Affordability is always affected by supply and demand. A booming property market might be welcomed by some, investors and government alike, but the reality is that a stable and affordable market is better for the public, the workers, business owners and the country as a whole.

WHAT ARE YOU DOING WITH YOUR MONEY?

Perhaps you have a reasonable family income. What are you doing with it? Well, there are a few choices, including:

- Overspending, including increasing your credit card debt as you live beyond your means. Forced to work a 60-hour week that makes you neither happy nor helps to make ends meet.

- Saving in a bank or building society, maybe even purchasing bonds. However, rates are so low that inflation is effectively countering any gains you might be making.

■ Doing okay and starting to think that clearing your mortgage is a good idea.

Uncertainty caused by the exit vote has influenced the spending decisions of much of the population. People are choosing not to enter or to leave the UK. Companies are considering relocating their headquarters and production to avoid currency fluctuations and tariffs. This is all bad news for the economy as a reduction in consumer spending and increased unemployment could trigger a recession!

It is crucial to review all our spending habits, of course, and to teach our children about money, debt, credit cards, credit scores, and the influence interest rates have on business and the economy.

On the other hand, interest rates are in a record low phase. So leaving money in an account or bond where it is earning less than the rate of inflation is like filling a bath without putting the plug in. Your money will not grow and, in real terms, will actually be worth less as the cost of living increases.

Maybe it's time to consider investing in property as a way to make your savings work harder and generate more income for the family. While a property a long way from home may not make sense as a future home for your children, plenty of families do not think twice about buying random properties that are based on where their child chooses to study.

Maybe it's time to create a property investment strategy which highlights where your money would generate the greatest return, one which could create more family income to be used for whatever purpose you choose.

THE AVERAGE PERSON IN ENGLAND STILL WANTS TO OWN THEIR OWN HOUSE

The average person is still striving for some past ideal where an 'Englishman's home is his castle'. Some say it started with Margaret Thatcher's ideals, but I know my parents held those beliefs some 20–30 years before she came into power.

As a country, we have this conflict between feeling our 'home is only our castle if we own it' and yet seemingly being priced out of the housing market.

Home-ownership was much less common in the early part of the last century. Many people survived on just the average wage for the time and so were only able to rent their homes. Pension income was small, if there was any at all, so people were forced to keep working. Then, when they were unable to work any-more, people were forced to rely on their family for support.

By the latter part of the 20th century, owner-occupation had expanded and home-ownership had become a source of both security and status, thanks to new Conservative policy. The goal was to buy as soon as possible in adult life, and then pay off the mortgage on a 25-year term, long before retiring debt-free. Older people could survive on the income from the state pension, and pass on the value of their property to their families.

Today, owning a home is still a source of security and status. Although many people defer on making such a large purchase.

The Council of Mortgage Lenders (CML) shared the outcome of their research in early March 2017. The premise was flawed as it came from this ancient belief about home ownership. So many young people are focused on travelling before saving for a deposit that needs to be matched by massive debt. This represents settling down, growing up, the end of fun and good times. The CML predicts that future generations will delay buying their first homes and rent for longer.

My daughter's friends took their inheritance from their family and spent six months travelling in the Far East. A life-changing experience. Now they are back in rented accommodation. Yes, because they can't afford to buy, but that is because their priorities and values are different. They valued travelling over staying put.

The other thing that the CML shockingly got wrong was when they referred to people's houses as an asset.

The term asset, according to the Oxford Dictionary, means: "An item of property owned by a person or company, regarded as having value and available to meet debts, commitments, or legacies."

There is no definition of an income-generating asset – which is exactly what a buy to let property is! If the dictionary can't tell you, then there is no hope!

Therefore, claiming that older people use their homes as "an asset to be drawn upon to supplement a modest retirement income" is blatantly wrong. The house would have been an income-generating asset if they had re-mortgaged it while they were still working and then reinvested the capital into income-generating property assets.

The best thing about viewing property through my eyes, as a professional property investor, is that I understand I neither need to own the home I live in nor live in any of the homes I own. However, the properties we do own must pay for us to live rent-free in a home of our choice. This means that the implied challenge of stepping up on to an unaffordable housing ladder is removed for first-time buyers. Instead of buying where you currently want to live, but can't afford, invest where you can afford and let the rental profit start to offset the cost of renting a property where you want to live.

Let me explain this further so that you can start to detach yourself from the beliefs which served your parents in post-war Britain. More importantly, to refrain from passing these on to your children.

We already know that our lives are becoming more mobile. We move for work, for pleasure or out of aspiration, while some stay put because of family ties. The lives of our children will be driven by their desire and need to be more mobile, more flexible and generally less attached to one physical place.

They may start by needing to relocate for study, then for work and eventually, when love strikes, for family reasons, but they are more likely to move out of choice due to advances in technology. So the dilemma of where they will call their home needs addressing in another way. What if you could have the benefit of feeling secure without the burden and obligation of a residential mortgage on a property which may no longer suit your needs?

What if you or your children (over the age of 18) owned a number of properties in a part of the country where the rental income was high in proportion to the purchase cost of the property? What if rental income gave you the flexibility and choice to live wherever you wanted? So, while you are young, single and working in the city centre, you choose to live in a flat in town. Then, as you meet a partner, settle down and start a family, you want a garden, so you move. Finally, as you retire you move to the coast, and this is all done without the cost and stress of selling a single property!

THERE IS A CHALLENGE WITH RENTING

Part of the challenge as a tenant in the UK, is that we currently use six-month AST (assured shorthold tenancy) agreements as our contractual agreement, developed through the housing acts of 1980, 1988 and 1996.

In Germany, for example, the majority of property is rented accommodation. 90% of properties in Berlin and 80% in Hamburg are rented. The primary contract in Germany gives a tenant an unlimited contract to rent, and even if notice is given by a landlord, a tenant can still appeal to stay. Combined with the lack of an appreciable rise in house values, this makes for a much more stable and secure housing market. Tenants have rights around rental increases and compared with London it's almost 50% cheaper to rent in Munich.

For the average tenant in this country, the message is: 'Live here for a while – I don't expect you to stay long because this is not really your home.' It is no wonder private renting here is only at 20%. Whereas in Germany, the message is: 'Stay as long as you want – you are welcome.' Needless to say, properties in the UK can often be treated as temporary homes, maintenance costs can be high and turnover is expected, especially in the city centres. In Germany, tenants are expected to pay for the cost of redecoration, more like a commercial lease.

If you add the fact that the German housing market has only risen about 2–3% in the last ten years, during which time housing prices have almost doubled in the UK, then maybe the problems with the housing market have less to do with Margaret Thatcher and more to do with property speculation and inappropriate tenant/renting legislation.

HOW CAN WE CHANGE THE VIEW OF RENTING?

We need to separate the idea of owning properties and living in a home. Yes, we do still have a bit of a challenge in the UK with the AST contract, but if asked, professional landlords would all state the same fact: 'We would love a long-term secure tenant.'

Maybe I am jumping ahead with these radical ideas a bit too soon – I just want to shake up the way that you think and say it doesn't have to be like this. If you start now, you could create a cashflowing portfolio of properties that generate additional income for you and your family. Depending on your needs, it could fund school fees, university fees, a deposit for a house, pay the rent on a city pad for you or your city-working offspring or fund your retirement.

It can be done. I will show you examples: one where you can take control, especially if your children are under 18 and therefore not yet eligible for a mortgage. I will also show you how you can help your teenager prepare to buy their own home, or property portfolio, as soon as they get a full-time job and pass the legal requirements to hold a mortgage. I will explain to you in easy-to-follow steps how I taught my daughter to buy her own £200,000 house in Greater London with no money from the 'bank of Mum'.

Since the start of 2009, I have bought enough houses to generate sufficient funds to mean that I no longer need to work to earn money. I have used this experience to help bespoke clients to buy investment properties which have enabled them to do everything from giving up work and starting to design children's books to emigrating to a life in the sun, while leaving behind a portfolio of cashflowing properties which take care of the family in their absence.

I regularly speak at both property and business-related events, sharing my knowledge and understanding. As more people asked me to help them, I started to write books (this is my third in a series of titles) and I now mentor a small number of private clients to grow their business in property or commerce. The bulk of my business is helping people to invest in cashflowing portfolios.

Throughout everything I do, my passion for life and learning is, I believe, evident. I love to share my knowledge; it is my books, talks and businesses that enable me to do this. We don't have to work a 60-hour week to make ends meet. We have the income that gives us the freedom to choose to live our lives on our terms. In a sense, I am living a Non-Traditional Retirement, something I explain in more detail in my next book.

Best of all, I have made every decision that brought me to this point. I recognised that I needed to take responsibility for my financial life quality and it was going to be fun all the way. Most importantly, when the time to slow down does eventually arrive, I will not be a burden on my children. I will not compound their debt. I will not limit their lives by making them sell everything they have to pay for my living and care costs.

We have been repeatedly fed the same myths – by our schools, the government, the media and, unknowingly, by our parents. It's time to get the truth out into the open and really start to recognise the mess we are in – and us with it! It's time to take steps to secure your financial future now that you know where you stand.

Let me ask you some questions as a way to summarise what I have covered already:

- Do you have children or plan to have children, and do you worry about how they will ever be able to afford to get on the housing ladder?

- Do you work hard and earn a good wage, yet there is never enough... enough time, enough money, enough fun?

- Are you worried that your pension will not be worth enough to support you in your retirement?

- Do you wish you could do something different, but can't afford to leave your job?

- Are you worried you might lose your job?

- Would you just like to know how you can feel more relaxed about money, feel wealthier and feel more positive about the future?

If you have answered yes to any of these questions, then investing in a cashflowing property portfolio could be the perfect solution.

Chapter 2 will unpack some of the myths which I believe are holding us back from a simpler and more secure financial future. A future that is secure because, as we become more successful and wealthy, we help others, reinvest in the economy and put fuel into the economic engine rather than watch it jerk through a repeating cycle of boom and bust.

We need to understand that the lives, learning styles, working conditions and priorities of the next generation are so very different from what we experience in our lives, as well as the demands that are placed on them. The speed of information, their ability

to multi-process and working practices are all changing dramatically with technological advances. The
dangerous state of our debt-ridden global economy
means that the chances of our grandchildren living
a comfortable and secure life are guaranteed to be
minute – unless we start making the changes NOW!

As you read on through the following pages,
leave your old ways of thinking behind. Be open to
new ideas and new ways of doing things. This is not
just for you but for your children and your families –
you need to understand how everything is changing
and how you can prepare.

CHAPTER

2

THE 7 MYTHS ABOUT MONEY WHICH WILL DISADVANTAGE YOU AND YOUR CHILDREN FOR LIFE

MYTH 1: WE DON'T NEED TO KNOW HOW MONEY WORKS – WE HAVE JOBS

FACT: YOU MUST UNDERSTAND HOW MONEY
WORKS. ANYONE WHO DOES NOT
IS HEADING FOR FINANCIAL DISASTER.

In fact, you need to think of yourself as a business, and then those around you will also start to think that way. What are your skills and how are you selling them? You may sell your skills to another person as an employee or contractor. Or perhaps you are selling an idea (as a product, concept or service) as a business owner with employees, contractors or outsourced staff.

This is the age of the micro-entrepreneur, even government policy and tax concessions are focused on the smaller business owner as a way to stimulate economic growth. There were 5.7million small businesses in the UK in 2017. 5.5m of those classed as micro-businesses employing under 9 staff. This accounts for 33% of all UK employment and 22% of turnover! This is a growth sector you could easily join! (Reference: House of Commons Library Briefing Paper #06152 December 2017 by Chris Rhodes.)

Your children will need to think more entrepreneurially because the idea of a job for life will not exist forever. With the average student leaving university with £50,800 of debt – once interest is factored in – and 5% of them joining the dole queue, it seems the world has gone mad. As a result, the next generation is getting online and working out how they can sell something – an idea, a skill or their time – to someone else; they are not waiting around.

So what has this to do with needing to know how money works? I believe we all need to think like business owners and know the value of our time or skill. We need to maximise the return we get from that exchange, either in terms of money, flexibility, stability, status or other values which are important to us.

We need to understand how to survive and pro- vide – to survive in a world built on debt and provide for our families. And by that, I mean to provide not just the cash resources but the knowledge and under- standing which traditional education simply fails to impart.

What do you and your children understand about money, credit and the real cost of interest pay- ments? Do you understand the term good debt versus bad debt? If our schools have not explained this, then how can we be expected to function in today's busi- ness world?

Do you realise the impact one missed mobile phone payment can have on a credit score? And do you understand how this can impact your future ability to buy a property? Do your children understand this?

Managing your credit scores and even your online reputation is crucial if you are to be even more successful in the coming years. How long is it before lenders check Facebook to decide whether they will lend to you? Employers are already known to check social media profiles, as part of their recruitment strategy. In fact, LinkedIn is, in part, a giant recruitment marketplace.

Truth

We cannot carry on blindly following the advice that was offered in school – it is outdated and behind modern times. This advice was to:

1. Buy a house on a mortgage and live happily ever after. You can't.

2. Rely on the government to keep you safe, fed and housed – there is plenty of money. There is not.

3. Debt is good. It is not good if it is spent on liabilities rather than assets. Only the lender benefits from the interest payments you make to them.

4. Your pension will be fine – just save more. It will never be enough; you will live too long!

5. Go to university and get a good job. No, you won't. You will just get another £50,000 debt to pay off. No wonder you have to move home and live with Mum and Dad!

MYTH 2: THE GOVERNMENT WILL TAKE CARE OF YOU

FACT: WITH AN AGEING AND EXPANDING POPULATION, THERE JUST IS NOT ENOUGH MONEY TO GO ROUND!

Since the introduction of Beveridge's welfare state in 1942, the government has been driven by the need to take care of us. Each successive government over the last 70-plus years has worked even harder to give us the impression that it can afford this commitment.

Beveridge's aim was noble and politically astute. The country needed a healthy, educated population living in decent housing that could go out and do a hard day's work, getting the nation and the economy back on its feet after the devastating human and financial cost of the Second World War. So, creating jobs through a national health service (NHS), free education system, planned building works and various other government bodies, increased employment, generating a flow of money, which stimulated the economy.

The rebalancing of the economy came at a cost: income support through unemployment benefit, sick benefit plus free education, free housing, free healthcare, including prescriptions, glasses, dentistry, operations and general health practitioners – the cost is enormous.

Between 2009–2010 the government spent £671.4 billion despite tax revenues of only £496.1 billion. This rose to £701.7 billion in 2010-11 and the figure was £761.9 billion in 2016-17. Ironically, the last time we borrowed on this scale was to fund the Second World War.

The downside in economic terms of a healthier population living longer, because of the free and life-prolonging treatments of the NHS, is the burden on the other social services.

As adult mortality has decreased, the average age men and women live to has increased. After the Second World War, when the state pension age was 65 years for men, their life expectancy was 66.4 years, while women's was 72.5 years. In fact, men today typically live to 77, while the figure is 82 for women.

By 2056, the life expectancy of a man and woman living in England is expected to be 84 and 89 respectively. What is the extra cost in terms of pensions, healthcare, supported living? Is the government making provision, building the care homes and hospitals to support this population?

For the first time in history, Britain's over 65 population outnumbers the under 16-year-olds, which is a bad omen for future tax revenues – a sure sign of even greater budgetary problems ahead if we maintain this course and live a subsidised existence.

The benefit system, which was designed to support those most in need, has since created a culture of expectation and dependency amongst the generations to follow. I have met many young people who are part of a long line of unemployed and disadvantaged families – often with parents who are separated, poor and suffering from addictions.

I was tempted to say they lack motivation, but that's not accurate; they lack something to be motivated about. The possibilities in their lives have been limited by their parents' and grandparents' lack of employment. This new generation of young parents is no more capable of holding down a job or teaching their children about a bright new future than their grandparents were.

Some young people develop the belief, through the media and peer pressure, that reliance on the state is acceptable. Many live on the edge of a black economy. Those with entrepreneurial skills learn to survive on benefits by identifying ways to generate additional income and opportunities. They have found a way to survive which effectively empowers them rather than leaving them feeling powerless and impoverished. The majority of young people are entrepreneurial and creative, but a series of life events has meant they do not feel empowered to work within the system and don't recognise that relying on the benefit system is part of their problem.

The costs of all these outbound payments are met by taxes, and when the potential burden of tax required is too high, then the government resorts to borrowing. This, in turn, becomes our national debt.

Just as in a family unit, if you keep spending on pensions and NHS, free education and unemployment benefits at a rate higher than you are earning through taxes, for example, and resort to borrowing or creating more 'cash' through fiscal measures with no clear plan to repay the debt, you will soon be in trouble. That is our national situation. We are in trouble. Successive governments have spent more on social care than we can afford.

Now our government ministers are distracted by global politics and a changing political landscape as other European countries express a form of popular rebellion through their voting systems. Our home-grown criticisms of policy, or a lack of it, are multiplying. This will only result in another backlash and its associated crippling burden of debt, which will pass down the generations.

So what does the myth that 'the government will take care of you' mean to us and, more importantly, our families? Will it mean debt and disaster, unemployment and global recession, a lack of money, hunger, and maybe even civil unrest? Greece has been a perfect example of this madness; because they could not pay their debt, Europe lent them more money... surely this madness is evident? The real irony of all this is that I first wrote that sentence in 2012, in the first edition of this book, and it remains unedited six years later!

This book is not designed to solve the political or financial problems looming on the horizon, but rather it is here to help you recognise the potential impact on your family and how you can make changes now to set course for a more financially secure future.

In truth, all you need to know in this context is that you will have to start doing things differently. You and your family will have to take responsibility for your own financial futures and then, when you have mastered your own financial situation, help those around you.

There is a growing culture which desires change and a new way, rather than a black market or a grey economy way. People are coming together in partnerships to lend one another money in a different way. Why leave your money in the bank if you could lend it to a family member or friend and get better interest, or even a reward in another format? That is how I bought part of my property portfolio.

Crowdfunding *Dragons' Den*-style and 'Angel' funding are obvious examples of how to borrow money without going to the bank. Thanks to technology and the rate of innovation, ways of doing business are changing rapidly.

Individuals are finding how technology can help them get their projects funded and others are finding a more satisfying return on their savings than the paltry 2-3% in the banks. Online environments, like Crowdcube and FundingCircle, to name a few, enable people to lend money to one another.

The micro-entrepreneur earns money from their knowledge, skills or possessions. Uber and TaskRabbit, as well as sites that rent out your parking space or spare room, like Airbnb, are evidence of this, showing how everything our parents took for granted, including a job for life and a guaranteed pension to live on, has changed.

Truth

The government is going bankrupt trying to pay for an ideal promise made 70 years ago. It is unsustainable. The truth is, pensions will be worth nothing in the future, whether you are relying on a state pension or a private pen-sion. You need to act now and secure a financial future for your family.

MYTH 3: WORK HARD, BUY YOUR HOME AND LIVE HAPPILY EVER AFTER

FACT: YOU WILL HAVE TO SELL YOUR HOME TO AFFORD TO EAT; YOUR HOME IS NOT AN ASSET.

I don't know if I explicitly learnt this at school or if it was implied by my parents, but I expected to get a job, buy a house on a mortgage, pay it off over the next 25 years and live happily ever after.

Even as I was working for a mortgage company in my early life, I could see how the model I described above didn't work. Homebuyers needed to take out a 'savings/life' policy called an endowment that would mature and pay out a lump sum designed to clear the mortgage debt because the monthly payments required were too high when calculated over a 25-year term. My daughter's mortgage payments are spread over 35 years! In Japan, mortgage debt is passed down to the next generation – is that what you want for your family?

Back in 1983, mortgage affordability ratio was 3:5, meaning the average property (£31,203) cost 3.5 times the average salary (£8,902). By 2007, the average house price was £199,084 and that represented over 5.8 times the average person's salary (£34,252).

The average property price had doubled in just seven years from £31,203 to £68,623 by 1990. By 2003, 13 years later, it had doubled again to £132,371. Between 2003 to 2007, in just four years this time, average property prices rose by 150% to £199,084. This meant that property was increasing in cost by £45.69 a day! Or £1,370.82 a month!

When prices rise that quickly, a crash is sure to follow. It did! It was the start of a ten-year deep recession. Even now, post-recession and before a new cycle of house price rises, the average price of a semi-detached house is still £225,674 a 13% rise in a recession.

The financial crisis meant that some people were changing their mortgage products from capital and repayment, the traditional way to pay off some of your debt, to interest-only payments to reduce the monthly cost, as they struggled to make ends meet. This meant they were paying a mortgage on a property which they will never own because 20 or 30 years from now they will still owe the same debt. They were gambling that high prices will rise and interest rates stay low enough so that they can avoid repossession! Lenders are starting to change their policies to avoid the chaos you can imagine happening if this practice persists.

Ironically, I use that same method to buy my property portfolio. I focus on paying the minimum repayment to the bank through an interest-only mortgage in order to maximise the cashflow and profit from the property. Ultimately, when the time is right, I can sell the house to clear the original debt or choose to make overpayments to clear down the loan.

I also expect property inflation to increase the price of the property and effectively reduce the ratio of debt, which could enable me to sell one house to clear the debt from another two or three properties. At least I do it knowingly and as part of a business plan which generates cashflow for me and my family, rather than thinking I own my own home when actually I am just a high rent-paying tenant of a bank!

As I started to work with more clients to help them buy property that would generate an income, I began to see an equation forming.

During the course of your life, starting with birth and ending with death, you will most likely get a job and buy a house. We already know from historical data that house prices go up and even double in most cases in just over 7–10 years.

So, let's say you own your house worth £300,000 now and maybe it takes 10 years to double. In 2028, or thereabouts, your house could be worth £600,000. Your children will have left home and you might be thinking about retirement. Your government pension is worth nothing, your company or private pension is tiny because it has effectively lost all its value as stock market shares prices tumbled through economic uncertainty and corporate bankruptcies.

You consider selling the house – downsizing – but you will still need to live somewhere, so you buy a smaller house which has also doubled in price over the last 10 years and it costs you £400,000 to buy it. It's okay though because you own your house outright having paid off the mortgage – right?

So after selling and buying – let's not worry about calculating the cost of that right now – you have around £200,000 left to fund your retirement.

How much will you need to budget for a year to cover utility bills, insurance, food, clothes, fun and treats? How much does it cost you to live for a year right now? Use today as a reference... £20,000 per annum or £30,000?

Let's say you can survive on £20,000 a year – you don't eat as much now that you are older. You are probably still only 50–65 years, there is plenty of life in you yet – unfortunately. I forgot to ask... how long were you planning to live after you retired? Was it just 10 years? Oh, that's okay then, you can afford that!

If you need more than £20,000 per annum, and you will, or you live longer than 10 years – let's hope so – then, to put it politely, you are stuffed. You will have to sell the smaller house you bought to fund your life and it's only a basic life. If you or your partner needs special care, want a holiday or need to buy a new car – you can't! Is this the life you planned?

The cold hard fact is that as things stand now you will not get a mortgage again, because either you have already retired or because you only have 5–10 years before you retire and you simply cannot afford the repayments. If you don't sell this smaller property, then you will have to agree to a reversionary mortgage scheme, which releases money from your home to help you afford to live – but the cost is to your family and your legacy.

These reversionary mortgage schemes are already widely available and most involve you selling your home, your family's inheritance, to an insurance company in return for cash and the right to live there until you die. It's a great way to avoid inheritance tax...

you won't have an inheritance to leave! Is this the life you want after 40-50 years of hard work?

So, who will step in and save you? Not the government – they are broke. Let's hope you have children because they are going to have to buy everything for you.

There is no point even trying to imagine how your children will cope when they want to retire. They will have used up all of their resources to support their ageing parents – that's you. Who will take care of them when, in effect, they have even less? They were born bankrupt and didn't even know it. Each new child starts life owing £17,000 for our overspending, greed and stupidity. Isn't it time we turned that around?

Where we look to our parents to pass down a mortgage-free property to us, your children will have no property of their own as they sold it to pay for your retirement after you sold everything you had!

It doesn't have to be this way.

Truth

There is such a thing as 'good debt' – where money is leveraged through a bank, or another form of lending, to buy assets, such as property. These assets then make a profit to pay the cost of borrowing and create an income for the investor. It is what I have done and what my clients are doing with me. In Chapter 3, Lesson 3 on page 127, I take the scene I described

above and show you how you can fund your retirement and that of your children.

MYTH 4: IF YOU SAVE FOR YOUR RETIREMENT OR HAVE A PENSION YOU WILL BE FINE

> FACT: ALL STOCK MARKET PERFORMANCE
> IS SPECULATIVE. INTEREST RATES HAVE
> DROPPED AND SAVINGS INTEREST
> IS PLUMMETING.

If you get smart about your investment strategy, then
some property investment strategies easily return over
10%-15% on your cash invested, after increased stamp
duty costs over five years. That means if you put the
same pot of money in a building society account, you
could potentially earn 2%, whereas property would
return 10-15% and, in time, there would be capital
growth as well.

Do you have a private pension? Have you looked
at how much it would pay out on retirement? We looked
at my partner Bob's pension to get a sense of what was
happening. Apparently, his pension is a high-performing pension with generous employer contributions.
Look at these shocking figures:

The £150,000 pension pot would result in

£7,200 per year family income. That is either food or heating and light – we couldn't afford both. If I took the lump sum and invested it in property using the simple model below, watch how the returns can grow:

By using mortgages, £150,000 could buy two properties worth £120,000 each.

The two tenants pay rent and after the mortgage and potential costs are deducted, the monthly profit would be 2 x £350 – that's £700 per month. That's £8,400 per year – already more than the pension would pay out.

Now consider that Bob cannot retire for approximately 25 years. The dates keep moving as people are forced to work for longer.

25 x £8,400 = £210,000 in rental income from just two properties.

What if you saved the income from the properties and bought more. What if you changed some of your spending habits and started to invest?

Now before you get too excited, there are conditions to drawing money from pensions. The money can only be invested in commercial businesses or investments. One financial advisor and pension expert explained to me that to have a reasonable income of £30,000 per year pension, you would need to have a pension pot of £1,000,000.

I worked out that at the current rate of contributions, Bob would need to work for sixty-six years, if we assume that his pension has been accumulating at

£15,000 per working year. So never mind the press reports and government legislation, the reality is that without our property investments Bob would not be able to retire until he was 111 years old – if he lived that long!

Truth

So, based on the numbers, the myth is busted. Most people think they have a pension and they are all right, but have you checked what your pension might be worth?

The second problem many people have experienced is that the majority of pensions are invested in the stock market, which has been performing unreliably for years. Even your savings are being eaten up by price rises caused by inflation. How long do you want to wait to retire? And what kind of life do you want to live when you do?

MYTH 5: THERE WILL ALWAYS BE AFFORDABLE HOUSING

FACT: GOVERNMENT FUNDED AFFORDABLE HOUSING IS AN UNSUSTAINABLE MODEL. THERE IS NOT ENOUGH TAX OR LAND TO KEEP BUILDING HOUSES TO RENT OR SELL BELOW MARKET RATES. YOUR CHILDREN

WILL NOT BE ABLE TO ACCESS THESE
SCHEMES UNLESS THEY QUALIFY.

The cold hard fact is we live on a small island with a growing and ageing population which needs somewhere to live. Sixty-three percent of existing properties are privately owned, with a further 4.7m (20%) owned and rented out. The private rental sector (PRS) provides more accommodation than Local Authorities. There are currently four million properties classed as social or affordable rental dwellings.

As properties become vacant, under the current plans, councils are being forced to sell all their properties that are in the top third most expensive price range compared to the same property size in the local area. The government estimates this will lead to 15,000 council house sales and raise £4.5 billion each year.

This money would be used to:

- Pay off historic debt incurred in building the council homes sold

- Pay for Right to Buy discounts for housing association tenants

- Pay for the creation of a £1 billion, five-year brownfield decontamination fund

- Pay for the building of a new 'normal affordable home' in the same area

The continuing government policy to forcibly sell off social housing stock will have a dramatic effect on tenants, uprooted and evicted, and is strongly opposed by Shelter.

There is not enough money, either from taxpayers, the government or the lenders, to fund the builders to renovate and build new property on the scale required. We are suffering from a housing shortage or rather property mismanagement, with 10,000 of empty and derelict houses in the areas outside major cities centres. While inside city centres, foreign investors are buying for capital gain and so do not bother with collecting rent or tenant management, preferring to leave the property empty and unused.

According to the latest estimates, there are over 930,000 empty homes in the UK, with a third of those left empty for more than six months. It is clearly a scandal – but also an opportunity.

At the moment, 26.1% of the population (all aged under 40 years) can't afford to own their own homes, and home prices are too high in great swathes of the country. And this is when the housing market is in a slump and prices are, relatively speaking, low. What happens when house prices start to rise again? And they will because simple economic theory states that demand is greater than supply.

Will wages rise at the same rate?

According to the House Price Index, in the period 2003–2007, house prices rose by 50%; wages rose by 18%. Between 2009-2012 property prices fell and speculation slowed, so both property and wages saw a 2% increase.

So the increase in property prices increase is down to supply and demand issues, as well as speculation and other market forces. The opposite is true of wages. Yes, they rise, but they are limited by the impact on the cost of service or production, depending on the sector you work in. Each product or service will have its own supply and demand curves that affect price and these curves dictate the wages of the workers. So, rather than the item (house) increasing in value because of demand, the item (products or services) needs to generate a profit and so restricts wages. Houses don't need to generate a profit – in its truest use of the word – for anyone other than landlords.

Houses are an emotional item for most people. In fact, you may even think they are an asset when, in fact, they are a liability.

An asset is something which puts money in your pocket without the need for you to work; a liability takes money from your pocket even when you do work. Your house is a liability; your car is a liability.

So, where do you plan to live in the future and what will your family – both children and parents – be able to afford?

Truth

If you understand property as I do, you will recognise this as an opportunity. You can buy property now while the prices are still relatively low. Buy property as an investment vehicle, using the logic of your head, rather than as a home chosen with your heart. These properties can then be rented out in return for a profit, and that income can help you and your family live a more affordable life.

MYTH 6: OUR CHILDREN BELIEVE THEY CAN'T OR SIMPLY DON'T WANT TO INVEST IN PROPERTY

> FACT: PROPERTY IS A GREAT INVESTMENT THAT IS TANGIBLE, IN DEMAND, AND ALLOWS YOU TO HAVE DIRECT CONTROL OVER THE AMOUNT OF INCOME IT GENERATES.

There are two parts to this myth and they both have to do with how some people think. On the one hand, there are people out there who think it 'will all be okay' – that the government will take care of them and their children will be fine.

On the other hand, there are the doomsayers, e.g. those newspaper articles that constantly state how tough things are. Sadly, our children are being influenced by them. This book will present solutions and a way to think differently.

I believe the first myth will have shown you that it will not 'all be okay'. That the economy, in all its complex forms, will not sustain our lives – which are built on mounting debt – the way it has for the past 50-70 years. If banks still exist and if our children are eligible for loans, then they may need to borrow such an extraordinary amount of money, they will have no hope of repaying it in their lifetime. As a result, that property may become a burden that's passed down through the generations, with grandchildren continuing to pay for property bought by their grandparents.

This makes buying a property sound like a dangerous activity – I believe it is if you do not understand exactly what you are getting into by taking on that debt. If you do not have a plan to repay the debt, then, yes, it is dangerous and foolish.

What about the doomsayers? Are they right? Well, maybe they are for some people who follow the traditional approach to home ownership. I do not know you, the reader, personally, and I do not know your current financial position. What I do know is that we are failing the next generation, our children, and our grandchildren. We are allowing government decisions and our past spending habits to burden them with debt. Meanwhile, we deny them the knowledge and tools to change things. I do not offer financial advice, but I am passionate about sharing my financial journey and the understanding I have derived from that.

When I work with clients, I ask them to look at a number of resources they have (that we all have):

- How much time do you have? Do you work full time?

- How much cash or equity do you have to invest?

- What is your attitude towards risk versus perceived reward?

- What does your family consist of? How many children and partners, parents or siblings do you have?

- What kind of life are you looking to create for yourself and your family?

The answers to these questions help me to explain how it is possible to achieve a different outcome from those outlined in the newspapers. I am not alone, I have friends and clients who have achieved the same outstanding results: freedom from a job, funded by a property portfolio which gives them the choice to do what they want and run the businesses they choose.

On page 137, I explain, by using examples, how you can take your current assets (cash or equity) and invest in property in a way that will help you to gain financial freedom. I also explain in detail how you can help your children buy their own home or a collection of houses which give them the freedom to live where they want and work how they choose. And they won't have to wait until they are 35 years old to achieve it either!

Truth

The truth is that the specific solution will be different for everyone, but the broad principle is the same.

By the end of this book, you will be more aware of the financial resources you have access to, and you can always go on to read *Using Other People's Money; How to invest in property* to extend this knowledge. By the end of this book, you will think differently about income and assets, the value of money and how to leverage it so that you have just what you need to cover your cost of living.

As you share the lessons in this book, your family will learn about money, debt, assets and liabilities. They will learn lessons not taught in school. They will graduate with a property portfolio which provides a secure baseline of income to enable them to go on to create wonderful lives, possibly discover new medical treatments, technological advances, create works of art or music or become amazing athletes – become whatever they choose because they can. Meanwhile, you will be comfortable in your retirement, which you perhaps took early. You will certainly neither be a burden to your children nor reliant on the government for handouts.

MYTH 7: LISTEN TO YOUR TEACHERS, LISTEN TO THE GOVERNMENT – THEY KNOW BEST

FACT: HARDLY ANY SCHOOL TEACHERS ARE SUCCESSFUL PROPERTY INVESTORS, YET MOST GOVERNMENT MINISTERS OWN TWO PROPERTIES – WHAT ARE YOU NOT BEING TOLD?

Having been a teacher myself at college and university, I know the majority of teachers do an amazing job. The problem with education is that it is out of step with the modern world and shackled by government legislation and targets.

If you want to be a successful athlete, who would you watch or want to train with? If you want to be a race car driver, who would you want to teach you? If you want to know about the universe, whose books would you read?

If you want to know how to make money and be successful in business or property investment, would you ask a schoolteacher?

We are bound and limited by the people around us, their experiences, their beliefs and their ideas. So does this mean that if we mix with inspirational and successful people, we will be inspired and become successful? I believe so.

Think about the people you mix with and the conversations you have. Are your conversations about your collective worries about money? Do you talk about what you lack and do not have enough of? Are your conversations predominantly negative?

Think about what this does to your mind. If all your talk is negative, then your subconscious mind will look for information (the millions of gigabytes we process every day) that reinforces your beliefs.

Look around the room, train or wherever you are reading this book. You have 30 seconds to count how many blue objects you can see. Now close your eyes and tell me how many red things you saw? You can't because you were focused on the blue. Yet, the red things are there too if you look for them.

What about a different type of conversation: the drama of other people's lives? This includes listening to the news and reading magazines that are full of stories of so-called celebrities (who they are dating, divorcing, etc.). What do you watch on television? Now, just to be clear, I like television. I watch dramas and crime programmes for entertainment, but I don't watch programmes that revel in the misery of others.

Then there are the conversations where you take ideas and grow them; you explore new learning or share insights. Personally, I enjoy watching debates and discussions on the economy. I like to talk about developments in business and thinking. I like to talk about property deals.

I can also have fun and relax – I am not too boring to go out with. I just don't want to spend my time discussing what happened during a miserable television show, the latest tragedy involving a child or the latest political or celebrity scandal. Fortunately, neither do my friends. Every one of them is fascinating and fun and I enjoy their company.

Truth

I have learnt more about life since I left school, and I have used this new knowledge more effectively than I did in solving any maths equation. Don't misunderstand me; I totally agree that we need to learn the basic skills of maths and English. However, even though I have two degrees and taught at University for years, I am not convinced that a business degree is worth three years of anyone's life, let alone £30,000 of debt! I do believe this would be better invested in property!

Work out what you want in life and then look for (research if you need to) people who are successfully living the life that you would like to move towards. Work out what they have done and read their books, listen to them speak. Take a chance to work with them if you can. It's called 'modelling'. Get better and more relevant teachers.

SUMMARY

If the seven myths have done anything, I hope that they have helped you to see that you need to think differently.

➡ Do you still think the government can support you in a retirement you would like?

➡ Do you think that buying a family home gives you future security?

➡ Do you think paying off your personal mortgage is your current number one priority?

➡ Do you think your family will be able to afford their own homes?

➡ Do you think traditional education is keeping up with the pace of technology and is teaching your children how it will impact on the way future generations live their lives?

➡ Is the government explaining how they plan to effectively tackle the burgeoning economic debt?

➡ Do you think future increases in property prices will solve the economic crisis and your financial future?

➡ Do you trust the media, the government, the banks or your faith in the future?

➡ Do you think your children have the financial education they need?

If you answered no to the majority of the questions above, then please read on. If you answered yes, then please go back and re-read the myths. Do your own research and please come to your own conclusion. If you then decide to do nothing, at least you can't blame anyone for not telling you how bad things are or that you need to change the way you are thinking. A fundamental understanding of how money works is crucial because you are the head of your own family business, whether or not you realise it.

Chapter 3 looks at the seven lessons you and your family were not taught in school and how understanding them will change your life.

CHAPTER

3

THE 7 MOST IMPORTANT FINANCIAL LESSONS YOU WILL EVER LEARN

I want to turn education and popular belief on its head so that you can share your understanding with your children and teach them what education is failing to tell them. I want to help you and your family make decisions about your lives and property investment in a way that better suits how your children will interact with property in the future. I want to help your family prepare for, and thrive through, any oncoming economic turbulence.

I have made an assumption that you do want to provide for your family's financial future. Otherwise, you might not be reading this book. I want to make it clear that by understanding this new way of thinking about money, property and the coming shift in our economic future, you will also be preparing for your own financial future should you become redundant, want early retirement or decide to move on to set up your own business.

You could work through this chapter together with your family. Listening to your younger children and discussing what is important to them will give you incredible insight into parts of them you might not have recognised before. Children as young as four or five are already stating that caring for the environment is important to them.

We all go to school, theoretically, to get a good education. In fact, we are trained in a small sphere of knowledge which the government believes is important to us. What they are repeatedly missing is that the pace of knowledge and understanding is multiplying to the Nth degree. Our children get this, but the teachers and politicians of the older generations don't. The term 'education' comes from the Latin word to 'pull out' or 'draw out'. Do you feel your internal knowledge that was pulled out of you at school flowed from you?

Ask your children what they think – they are probably bored both with the content and the delivery mechanisms. They may not see the relevance of reciting the alphabet and times tables – you can help! The British education system is not preparing our children for life or the changing world of work in a global and digital economy. Young people are not taught about assets and liabilities, about income and expenses in a practical and tangible way.

This book will give you the tools to start your own financial revolution and break your dependence on the state system while contributing to the lives of your family, future generations and all the families and people that you house in decent homes.

You may have noticed that you do everything online – your access to information and the power to process it – is phenomenal. Education is a limiting factor, with its rules about spelling and grammar, individual work, even maths and languages. As a former university lecturer, I honestly believe we must help the younger generation identify what they need to learn, point out how easily they can learn it and what its benefits are. Then you can let them get on with it – because they are quicker and have access to more information than we ever had.

The greatest gifts you can give your children are the knowledge and the education to manage their money and ensure they invest it wisely in property and not the building society or designer clothes!

CHAPTER 3

The wealthy don't work for money – they make money work for them, and some people are better at doing this than others. Obvious examples of people who have mastered this skill are traditional business owners, big corporations and, of course, people like Lord Alan Sugar, Sir Richard Branson and hundreds of other well-known people. There are also thousands of smaller businesses run by successful business owners living great lives which they determine and control.

There are also people employed by businesses who love their jobs. They, too, have sold something they have – time – in return for money. Or maybe the satisfaction of a job well done, companionship or status. Even employees are small businesses in their own right, they just don't realise it.

So what are the seven most important lessons which you never learnt in school? Again, I am assuming you didn't take an accounting or economics degree, but even if you did, I might still challenge the status quo of traditional thinking.

In this chapter I am going to cover the following:

1. Lenders and how to get on their good side – a brief and simple history of banking and the money markets

2. Why money must keep moving

3. Leverage – making your money work for you

4. Why your savings are not worth a penny

100

5. Build a portfolio now

6. Letting go of old habits

7. Who is on your team?

In school, we are taught about currencies and denom- inations – not the history of the creation of money, how to use it and the alternatives. I am not going to delve too far into the future shape and use of money or cryptocurrencies, as that is an evolving book in its own right, but I will explore just far enough to shock you. Let's start with understanding lenders and how we got to be in the mess we are in...

LESSON 1: LENDERS AND HOW TO GET ON THEIR GOOD SIDE – A BRIEF AND SIMPLE HISTORY OF BANKING AND THE MONEY MARKETS

I want to explain a little about commercial lend- ing from my perspective and experience, and more about finance and lending in general. In 2009, when I approached my high-street bank to see whether I could borrow money from them to invest in property, I knew that I needed to understand how 'money worked'. I needed to understand their business model; what they needed from an ideal client, so I would be more lendable.

Moving to more commercial lending meant having conversations as a business client of the bank, which entailed a whole different language. It also sparked an interest in the whole system way beyond my previous understanding. I am not an expert, simply a keen student.

Without going back to historic times, money has been around the globe for thousands of years. It started with the use of tokens, like beads, stones and shells, as a means to trade unwanted or excess goods, products and services with another person or community.

Banks become a more formal institution as a place to store the gold that replaced shells and other artefacts as the preferred method of exchange. Paper money was initially a note which confirmed you had gold deposited in one store and it was easier to trade the paper note than the gold itself. That all sounds sensible but then, of course, there is always more...

Skip forward and the original gold deposit-style of banks was surpassed by private banks, which started to print notes and lend them privately. In 1694, during the reign of King William III and Queen Mary II, the Bank of England was established as the Central Bank of England. It was designed to act on behalf of the government during the war with France and was later nationalised after the Second World War in 1946. It's strange how wars and money are always so inextricably linked!

The creation of paper money and the rise of the private banks caused chaos as the value of the notes bore no real or tangible worth and were responsible for repeating cycles of inflation. In 1844, The Bank Charter Act meant that only the Bank of England could issue new legal tender in the form of notes and coins. Their aim was to control inflation and regulate the money supply through the Bank's direct link to reserves of gold. In effect, the rule was the bank could only print money for which it held an equivalent amount of gold unless there was a crisis, in which case they could change the rules!

Broadly speaking, there was an emergence of two sorts of banks. Firstly, consumer banks that collected savings deposits from, and lent to, ordinary people. These banks relied on and served the people who worked, accumulated personal surplus cash and then deposited it in the bank for safekeeping. This money was lent by the bank to other people for a fee. It was tangible real money and the bank only lent what it had. Second, there were investment banks, which were the accumulated wealth of a specific number of business partners who pooled their money and lent it to bigger projects and to businesses. Investment banks evaluated the risks carefully as they were lending their own money. This was still considered a more speculative form of lending with higher risks and rewards, based on longer investments in larger projects.

Financial innovation and the invention of derivatives flowed smoothly into the markets as the volume of lending exploded across the globe. Those working in banking found clever ways to invent and sell investments in what were effectively bundles of debt. Subprime mortgage lending in America quadrupled between 2000 and 2006 – we have all heard the phrase NINJA (no income, no job or assets) mortgages. This form of adverse lending against debt bundles is one of the reasons why Iceland and Greece became bankrupt and why Spain, Ireland, Portugal and Italy still teeter on the brink of the fiery pit.

The point of this chapter is to explain how we moved from a system of trade, which had a value, to a system of creating pretend money with no value which was then lent to other people (us) for a fee (interest). The interest then came back into the central pot and was lent out again.

The problem was, we were both borrowing and lending more than we had, which made the money worthless. Also, we were borrowing and lending it to people and countries that could not afford to repay the interest due. This meant the money was flowing in one direction and that was a very dangerous position for a system built on the flow of money (debt) and the payment of fees (interest).

To understand more about this history, and particularly the recent recessions and immediate causes and effects, you can read the papers and books produced by Raghuram Rajan, Eliot Spitzer, Satyajit Das and Charles Morris. For an easier, jargon-free read about why our financial system is doomed, read Simon Dixon.

So why have I written so much about the banking system? It is because our confidence and, therefore, our futures are linked to what happens across the globe now. The economy of one country affects all, as the complex web of loans and debts ensnare all who pass by, including you just minding your own business.

Ironically, in the section about credit cards on page 109, you will see how the general public has repeated the errors of governments and countries in their approach to borrowing, which is why so many people are struggling in debt, like mini-human Greeces.

You may have heard the comment that trillions of pounds are circulating around the globe at any one time. This is true, but it is digital debt – not real promissory notes backed up by tangible gold deposits. The problem is that instead of always lending real tangible money or paper notes backed by gold deposits held in vaults, banks now lend 4, 10 or 40 times the actual money they have to back them up. In recent years, you may have noticed that your credit card limits or bank overdrafts have been reduced without warning. This is because lenders will have technically promised you, in advance, that you can use that money if you need it. Now they need it; they want to lend it to other people for a fee, not have it sitting there 'just in case' you might want it!

What does the future hold? More of the same, sadly! No matter what Europe proposes in terms of regulation, America – with its powerfully placed advocates of high-risk, high-reward and consequences be damned, lending – will never agree. Obama, with a 'mandate for change', appointed the leaders of the original banking system, who created the crisis, to positions of power in order to change the current system. What do you think is going to change, if anything, now that Trump is in power?

We must regulate the production of money and reduce our reliance on debt. I believe the invention of cryptocurrencies is a revolt against a corrupt system, although recent trading cycles demonstrate that even cryptocurrencies are prey to the same morally corrupt practices of the monetary/banking system. By the end of this chapter, you will understand more about money and how it works so you can use it to acquire your own income-generating assets, even within the current debt-driven system.

We need to start the money moving at the bottom of the food chain again; we need to get spending personally and commercially, in a responsible, debt-free way that is calculated to promote business and commerce. We need to go around the outside of these major banks and investment houses to the private individuals with money. These people have also been failed by a system designed to support the 'uber-rich' on a scale that we cannot even comprehend.

Pensioners have lost their retirements and families their financial security. These same people are looking to both protect, grow and invest their remaining cash reserves to rebuild their financial futures. Maybe we can help one another, especially within our family groups?

Working around the system

When I started to research money and how it works, I realised that I could use the system to my own advantage – for the benefit of my family – and work around the system.

By understanding concepts like return on investment (ROI) and leverage (see Lesson 3 on page 127), I understand more about debt. I recognised that the system is broken, but I can also borrow money from the system – make it work for me. I can make sure that my money earns enough to pay the interest that I owe and then keep the profit as, in effect, my wage.

I can then also work outside the system and work with private money, non-banking, tangible non-debt cash. I can help others to leverage their assets and can use my surplus cash to fund other projects.

Like all lending, the most important thing before you start is to understand how much it is going to cost you to borrow the money when you can pay it back and who is going to pay the interest in the meantime. The biggest risk with borrowing money is the variable nature of the interest rate. This can be managed by either borrowing the money at an agreed fixed cost upfront or by developing systems to manage the risk – through monitoring and spreading it across your investment portfolio. I use a mixture of all of the above.

There is one other factor I would like to mention and that is the actual cost of borrowing in general. So much of the media is focused on the national Bank of England's base rate and how it is at an all-time low and set to stay relatively low.

What the press is not reporting loudly is that the mortgage companies borrow their money against something called LIBOR (London Interbank Offered Rate). This is currently averaging about 1% and climbing (GBP 6 month Libor rate). Ironically, even LIBOR is at the centre of a political and ethical debate. Whether or not this method of monitoring inter-bank lending confidence has to be replaced, remains to be seen.

In late 2017, the Base Rate rose a quarter of a percent and the impact on the housing market has been dramatic. First-time buyers pulled out of offers as they feared more rises, then vendors dropped off the market as they feared moving. Understandably, if you were going to take on significant mortgage debt (when buying a residential or investment property), then you would be foolish if you did not check that you could afford to still pay the mortgage if interest rates reached 5% or 6%. The new change to 0.75% in late summer 2018 will roll forward its impact into 2019 just in time for Brexit!

Are credit cards a safe form of financial tool?

While the section above is tangential to the under-standing of credit cards, I believe it serves as a great lesson in understanding the risk involved in borrowing money. However, there are also rewards if you 'play your cards right!' In its simplest form, a credit card, if used properly, can give you up to 45 days extra money – interest-free. In its most strategic form, it can lend you most of the deposit or costs for a property investment project at 0% interest for between 9 and 15 months!

Your challenge, with everything associated with borrowing money, is to understand the money flow of your deal. When you will pay it back, where that money will come from and who is going to pay the interest on the money while the project is being worked. The next challenge is how to borrow money on a credit card without affecting your credit score. Please be aware that lenders share financial informa-tion about you behind the scenes.

Banks want you to stay ignorant of the game and how it works. On the one hand, they want you to take out credit cards and buy stuff that you really can't afford so that at the end of the month you can't clear your credit card balance and instead pay them an exorbitant rate of interest because we are a debt-fuelled economy, as already discussed.

On the other hand, they now also want you to be a perfect borrower and require you to clear the debt in full. From a secured lending perspective, the underwriters of loans and mortgages need you to demonstrate that you know how to manage your money. One way that you can do this is to limit the amount of unsecured borrowing (credit cards) that you have available, clear your balances regularly, yet keep borrowing and paying back.

What you must understand is how a lender views the activity on your credit record and how this affects your credit score and, ultimately, your ability to borrow money through mortgages:

- Firstly, do not apply for too many credit cards at once or apply to have your existing cards increase their limits. Just by asking, you are affecting your credit score whether or not you are successful. Companies are now claiming that an application does not affect your credit score, but it might raise a flag to a potential mortgage lender!

■ Secondly, when you have cards, do not 'max them out' and use every last pound available to you, as you will look out of control and desperate for cash. Have a strategy to pay back your cards regularly and even overpay them now and then.

Credit cards are a brilliant tool for business owners and property investors; they act as a free overdraft and ease cashflow. They can also be leveraged by enabling you to buy stock and sell it for a profit before the interest or loan becomes repayable. In the dynamic financial climate in which we find ourselves, it is difficult to write any clear, hard and fast rules, other than to know what you are doing!

Credit scores – crucial to your financial future

Credit scores are a system of measuring your pre-dicted ability to repay a borrowed debt. If you intend to make your money work for you and leverage your assets, then borrowing money from somewhere is inevitable. Let's focus on the banks to start with and then move on to private lenders.

In the personal lending market, including small businesses, there are two primary agencies: Equifax and Experian. They keep records on you which you are entitled to review and challenge, if necessary. This includes personal data, such as where you live, whether you are registered to vote and a list of your financial associations. Financial associations mean anyone with whom you have entered into a joint financial commitment. This could be a personal loan, though more typically it would be a bank account or a mortgage.

Now, the person you are linked to influences how the lenders see your score. During a divorce, this can be how one partner becomes negatively impacted by the poor financial behaviour of the other partner, and this financial mud sticks. Next, comes a list of the loans or credit you have access to, for example, mortgages, personal loans, car loans and credit cards.

I noticed that my daughters had been receiving unsolicited post offering them a credit card at ridiculous interest rates of over 30–40%. So many young people will be tempted by this seemingly easy cash that they will not realise the true cost of the shoes or jumper they have bought until it is too late.

All our children have mobile, internet-active devices, along with their assorted contracts. The taking out of one of these contracts will have initiated a credit search and an entry on their credit report. If they miss a payment, even one, their future credit history is damaged for up to a year or more. Just £30 can ruin a credit score!

Missing payments is perceived as the first step to financial problems, either through lack of management and organisation or through lack of funds and over-commitment. Either way, it is frowned upon and penalised.

Gearing is another measure that a lender uses to gauge your suitability for borrowing. This is based on how much you have actually borrowed, particularly on unsecured lending like credit cards, against how much available credit you have. If you are highly geared, for example, you have one card which is near to its credit limit, then a lender may view you as living beyond your means, meaning that you could be at risk of defaulting.

You need to create and maintain a position where you are borrowing under 50% of your potential borrowing, and so have a gearing ratio of less than 50%. How do you work this out? Add up the total debt on all your credit cards and divide it by the total of all your credit limits.

I have guessed the figure of 50%. When I first increased my credit cards to cover my property training costs, my credit rating dropped through the floor. I called the credit agencies and spoke with them – they can be very helpful. They explained about gearing and I started to experiment by paying off my 0% credit cards bit by bit as they came to the end of the life of the offers. I noticed that my credit rating started to improve as my gearing ratio moved towards 60%. Of course, other factors will have been at play, such as the number of searches on my record, but I do believe gearing is now a significant decision-making factor.

So, the trick to managing your credit score is similar to managing your credit cards:

1. Know what you are doing and keep a record.

2. Keep your overall borrowing low relative to the amount you could borrow.

3. Again, set up direct payments for the minimum amount to avoid missed payments and make sure you have the funds to pay.

Social media score versus credit score

Think about how your lending looks to an agency whose job it is to score you. Do you look like a risk? Are you constantly applying for loans and credit cards? Think carefully and manage wisely for as long as you want to borrow from the establishment! Have you explained this to your children?

Of course, you could borrow funds from family, friends or a private investor – how would they check you out? Well, they could ask you to provide your credit score or they could just check you out online, through social media. That is going to be how decisions are made in the future. Your children uploading 'inappropriate' party photos with friends will find their history remains on the web forever. Future employers, business partners, lenders and friends will be able to trace your history and that of your children long after you have forgotten about a photo. Do you check what pictures your children or friends upload of you?

How many friends and connections do you have? How many blogs do you post? How many videos do you upload? How often do you interact with others online – sharing news and information – engaging in a debate? This bizarrely may matter in the near future as a sign of your connectivity and performance, even your contribution!

Once again, the point here is that time and technology are changing at an extraordinary rate and we need to keep aware and keep up! With a growing distrust of everyone, government and banking, lenders will need to qualify people who are suitable as potential borrowers. Maybe your social media score will more accurately indicate how successful you are likely to be than an arbitrary credit score. After all, true wealth is what you have that enables you to create wealth all over again once it is lost.

Interest and how your spending habits will send you broke

There are two final sub-lessons under this heading. The first is about how interest is often forgotten in the rush and passion of a purchase, which can result in the bargain costing more, much more, than originally perceived! The second is that spending cash from your capital pot, especially if it is not an income-generating asset, is actually madness.

Lesson 1 is about how money works; it is about interest rates and about credit cards. If your children do not know and understand how money works, then they are not only risking their credit scores, they are actually throwing away their hard-earned cash!

A purchase made on a credit card that is not paid off in the 'free' period actually accrues interest, daily. Over a month, this amounts to at a rate of at least 20% in most cases. Just borrow £5,000 and fail to clear the debt on an interest-accruing credit card and watch as £80 plus is added to your next statement. Every month that the debt remains uncleared!

This does not mean credit cards or loans are bad or something to be feared – it means they are tools which need to be mastered. An advanced lesson is to recognise the cost of borrowing and that what appears to be an opportunity or a bargain can actually cost a lot more when interest, fees and costs are included.

The only time a debt should remain uncleared past the due date on a credit card is when the interest rate is 0% and the purchase was related to an income-generating purchase. Without getting too preachy, the main problem with the debt many people are suffering today is that they bought items, often 'luxury' items, without considering how they were going to make the repayments.

This brings us to simple home accounts and budgeting. Having brought up two teenagers myself, and knowing how difficult it was at times to communicate with them, you may think I am mad to make this next suggestion. The important fact is that you can empower your children to understand about money, its value and how it can be leveraged by encouraging them to plan and monitor their expenses and savings for specific purchases. Maybe this involves using an Excel spreadsheet of their monthly expenditure. In fact, maybe you need that for your own household expenses. Maybe your children would prefer to use an app!

If you understand the benefit and advantages of keeping an account of your expenses and see it either as a game or a challenge, then it can be easier to motivate yourself. I had to keep a record of my spending when I was a single parent and really struggling on very little money. I learnt that if I managed my money really well, then I could actually get the bank to give me more money than I deposited – that extra £60–80 per annum of interest paid to me on my savings made a real difference to how we spent our summer holidays!

When my older daughter, Kimberley decided that she wanted to buy her own home, I explained how mortgages are calculated. More importantly, I explained the reality of how, as a future homeowner, you need to know that you can afford the repayments. She soon created a spreadsheet to help her understand how she spent her money and to see what was left each month. She noted how much she could save and what things she was spending on. That led her to reduce spending in certain areas of her life – or think twice about a purchase – so that she could reach her goal more quickly.

When Charlie, my younger daughter wanted to go travelling to South Africa, I explained to her how Excel worked and she drew up a spreadsheet to list all the expenses expected on her trip – her globe-trotting budget. Then, she worked out how much she could earn and how long it would take her to save her budget. Within nine months, she had saved her budget, flights were booked and she was walking through the departure gates at Terminal Five. She mastered budgeting so well that she extended a three-month trip to six months. Budgeting is now funding her six-year medical degree in Slovakia!

What do your children want or think they want to have or experience? By the end of this book, you will be able to show them how investing in property will help them to have everything they want and more besides! The passive income and greater return on their cash invested will help them to achieve their goals much sooner than planned. Best of all, they can then spend from the passively earned income and retain their capital invested to generate more income the next month, and then the next month and the next month.

The point here is to understand the difference between paying hidden interest on purchases made through credit cards or loans, instead of actually earning interest from investments that means you can spend for free. If the money earned is not spent, then it can actually start to multiply at a phenomenal rate.

This brings me to the impact of compounding interest. I have created two simple tables to explain my point. In Table 1, I have taken a one pound coin as an example and doubled it every day for 21 days...

Day	£ Compounded
1	1
2	2
3	4
4	8
5	16
6	32
7	64
8	128
9	256
10	512
11	1,024
12	2,048
13	4,096

14	8,192
15	16,384
16	32,768
17	65,536
18	131,072
19	262,144
20	524,288
21	1,048,576

Table 1: The Powerful Effect of Compounding

In the early stages of the experiment, nothing much happens as £1 becomes £2 and £8 becomes £16, but look where momentum starts to build at day 13 where £2,048 becomes £4,096 and then again at day 18 where £65,536 becomes £131,072.

Within 21 imaginary days, where you can double your money daily, £1 quickly becomes £1,000,000+.

Now consider Table 2 where you spend money on coffees instead of compounding the benefit…

Day	£ Spent	£ Accumulated and Compounded
1	2.75	5.5
2	2.75	13.75
3	2.75	30.25
4	2.75	63.25
5	2.75	129.25
6	2.75	261.25
7	2..75	525.25
8	2.75	1,053.25
9	2.75	2,109.25
10	2.75	4,221.25
11	2.75	8,445.25
12	2.75	16,893.25
13	2.75	33,789.25
14	2.75	67,581.25
15	2.75	135,165.25
16	2.75	270,333.25
17	2.75	540,669.25
18	2.75	1,081,341.25
19	2.75	2,162,685.25
20	2.75	4,325,373.25
21	2.75	8,650,749.25

Table 2: Assume a daily coffee costs £2.75.
In 21 days, you would have spent £57.75

If you look, the coffee costs £57.75 over 21 days. However, if instead of spending the money on coffee you actually saved it, and used the compounding process shown in Table 1, how much would you accumulate? Each day, your money would double and what you did not spend on coffee would be added to the pot as well. Hopefully, this makes you think about every penny that you spend. It certainly changed my spending habits – I mean, really, how many pairs of shoes or necklaces does one girl need?

Don't answer that! When you spend money, it's gone. When you invest it and make it work for you, you can ultimately spend considerably more!

The bottom line is that banks have lost lots of money in the past and they now need to make a profit. Some have massive business debts to repay the taxpayer! When you take out a loan, consider the cost of any lender fees alongside your interest rate and the term of the tie-in period of the loan. This is obvious when you are dealing with mortgages, but can also apply to loans and even 0% credit cards.

LESSON 2: WHY MONEY MUST KEEP MOVING

If you do not understand how money moves and what it costs, how can you access it, afford to pay to borrow it and ultimately make it work for you?

What are your thoughts about money? Underlying this question is the concept of abundance. This can apply to so many areas of your life. I know without a shadow of a doubt that you are one of the top 10% richest people in the world – simply because you are reading this book. Do you feel abundant? It depends what you use as a comparison, of course. The truth is you are rich in so many ways.

Let's think about water. Is water abundant? You know where to find it and how to gather it when you need to use it, mostly because we are spoilt by taps and Perrier. Yet, if you were about to cross the desert, would you learn even more about water – that precious life-preserving resource?

That is what money is – a precious resource. You need to learn about where to find it, how and when to use it. Understand the difference it makes when money is invested well, and the damage it can do when created en-mass, through Quantitative Easing. Notice its indirect impact on our planet through war, and all that comes with that.

In brutal terms, if money is really just debt that is actually costing you money – stay with me here – then you need to make it work; or you need to work, to pay back for the pleasure of having it. If you spend it, then not only do you no longer have it but you still owe someone else for it!

It may seem that the only 'real' money you have is the money that you work for. Here, you have definitely given something of value – your time – in exchange. What you don't know – and nor do I – is whether your employer has had to borrow money in order to pay you.

Regardless of whether or not you have any 'real' money, I suspect that very few people will be able to live within their means as our parents would have said we should. Most people will have debt in some form: their home mortgage, a car loan, outstanding credit card balance or a personal loan, possibly something bought on credit, like furniture.

That debt will be costing you and in Lesson 1 on page 115 I have explained how to convert that debt from a cost to an asset.

Let's stick with this second lesson and the need to make money move. If it sits still in your house as equity, for example, then it is actually shrinking in today's economy. Why? Inflation at the time of writing is averaging 2.2% (CPIH 12 month rate). House prices rose by 0.1% in April 2018 fuelled by a lack of property on the market – probably exacerbated by the base rate rise as well and normal seasonal fluctuations.

What does this mean to you? First of all, the value of your house is basically stagnant. Secondly, even if it has increased in price, it is decreasing in value when inflation is factored into the equation. And, thirdly, have you considered why you are holding on to it? So many people see a debt-free house as a form of security. I do understand – I thought that too until I realised that my house would never feed or clothe me!

Keeping your money working for you is essential – not just now in a recession which has lasted for over 10 years in real terms and may continue, but also as a way to supplement your income in your old age.

While you might not like the idea of increasing your debt, remember there is a difference between good debt and bad debt. As long as you invest any borrowed money into assets that generate a profit, then you can actually use debt to create money.

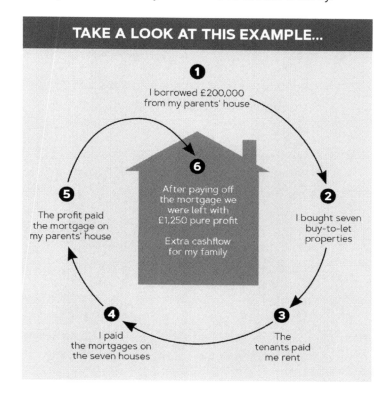

TAKE A LOOK AT THIS EXAMPLE...

1 I borrowed £200,000 from my parents' house

2 I bought seven buy-to-let properties

3 The tenants paid me rent

4 I paid the mortgages on the seven houses

5 The profit paid the mortgage on my parents' house

6 After paying off the mortgage we were left with £1,250 pure profit

Extra cashflow for my family

As the money moves around the circle other people benefit:

1. As I took out the loan, members of staff were employed to manage the transaction and a broker received a fee.

2. When the houses were bought, solicitors and surveyors were paid. Builders carried out repairs and refurbishments.

3. When the tenants moved in, insurance was taken out, fees were paid, members of staff were employed. Then the letting agency received a fee for managing the property. The tenant moved into a safe and decent home for their family.

4. As the rent paid first the smaller mortgages and then the main £200,000 loan, bank staff transferred and recorded money – creating more jobs.

5. The profit then moved into our bank account where it increased our monthly cashflow.

In the background, we employ a bookkeeper and a financial director. We pay for internet access and telephones. We drive cars and buy petrol. Our money fuels the economy and keeps people in work, as well as providing decent homes.

All this movement of money was fuelled by the original loan from the bank. Everyone in the chain has been paid and we still make a profit. Above all, it cost us nothing as all the costs were paid for using the money originally borrowed.

We actually got money for nothing. Well, that's not true: I worked out how to do this; I took a calculated risk and used my time and my knowledge to make it happen. The result, though, is long-term ongoing cashflow based on one day per month's work. That is how long I spend managing my property portfolio.

LESSON 3: LEVERAGE – MAKING YOUR MONEY WORK FOR YOU

Leverage is the process of taking an asset and enhancing its performance and outcome by applying a multiplier. By choosing property investment as my tool, I can leverage my money.

If, for example, I wanted to buy a house for £100,000 and I had that much in cash, I could buy the property outright. However, I could also get a loan from a bank, via a mortgage, for £75,000, according to current 'buy-to-let' lending conditions.

Let's ignore costs for the moment. In the first outright purchase, I would receive all the rent, ignoring insurance and letting agent fees for a minute. Let's say the rent was £500 per month or £6,000 per year.

In the second theoretical example, I could buy four properties at £100,000 each, using a mortgage of £75,000 and a £25,000 deposit on each one.

If I bought the four houses using four mortgages, I would obviously need to repay a monthly mortgage cost. This might be in the region of £75,000 at 3.5%/12 = £281.25 per month per property. Each month, I would make a £218.25 profit on each property, totalling £1,125 per calendar month and £13,500 per year – in effect, returning almost 225% more money each year than by owning just one property outright.

This is the power of leverage: splitting an investment and using other people's money for a sensible fee to increase the return on your investment so that everyone wins. This is how I became financially free in under two years and published my first book, called *Using Other People's Money: How to Invest in Property*.

So, if everything that you think of as money is actually debt, then it has to work to grow to beat the cost of inflation. When market conditions actually change, you can then watch as the rising prices reduce your debt and heighten your leverage even further. Look at this next example:

If we buy a £100,000 house using a mortgage of £75,000, the debt is £75,000. The buy-to-let mortgages are agreed on an interest-only basis. The debt is not reduced during the period of the loan as all the monthly payments are used to pay back the

THE 7 MOST IMPORTANT FINANCIAL LESSONS

interest costs and none of the capital borrowed, as it is in a residential, capital and interest mortgage. In 10 years' time – even 20 years – you will still owe the bank £75,000!

If you look at house prices since records began, you will see they have doubled on average every seven to ten years. So if we assume that it might take 10 years until the value of a property is worth double today's price, that means the £100,000 house would be worth £200,000 in 2028. The question is how much is the debt?

The answer is £75,000!!

This means that if you used leverage and bought four houses priced £100,000 each over the next 12 months and waited 10 years, you would have a property portfolio of £800,000 with only £300,000 of debt. That is a massive half a million pounds for doing nothing, plus you will have been receiving over £13,500 a year in rental income.

You should bear in mind here that this is an example I am giving to prove a point. I haven't included all of the costs that are associated with buying and have not included the management costs needed to ensure your portfolio is a high-performing asset, but I am sure you will agree that the principle is very exciting.

Imagine you made this investment for your eight-year-old child. They would then have all the income they needed to attend university. In fact, you could have paid for their private school education as well.

Imagine you have helped your 18-year-old child to do this. As a family, you would have considerable income from the portfolio – enough to pay the rent for your child to live where they choose, and enough to pay for you to live where you choose. You may also decide to leave home and turn your empty nest into a property shared by professional tenants for yet more income, while you go travelling.

Leverage has been applied to money to show how it works mathematically. It can also be applied to time. Whether you have a job or a business, you will be exchanging your time for money: profit or wages. Again, by using property you can buy a portfolio and then work less than one day per month to monitor it.

This depends on the size of your portfolio and the strategy you have used, of course. You will have a team of letting agents and builders if you need them.

The property will then generate your monthly profit over and over again – all for just one day's work per month. So, using the example above again, you could earn £1,125 per calendar for just a few hours' work, or maybe even just one hour a month, as that is all that would be needed for the four properties.

The property itself and the team around you have become the leveraging tool. That is why my busy clients use me to find, fix and fill their property portfolio. I have the knowledge and experience and also use (leverage) my time to save theirs.

While your home is not an asset and money must be kept moving to make money, you can also use other people's time to create the portfolio and, in doing so, turn your home from a liability into an investment tool.

LESSON 4: WHY YOUR SAVINGS ARE NOT WORTH A PENNY

In Chapter 2, myth 3 (see page 79) I explained that it was a fallacy to rely on your home as a future nest egg. Now I will take the lesson one step further and explain why your savings are not worth a penny and how you can make them work for you.

I will only touch briefly on the fact that your money is not that safe in a bank. Here are the reasons why:

- A run on the banks, as we saw with Northern Rock in 2008, will mean that you cannot access the notes if the bank cannot dispense them – as you are not in control. Some banking customers experience this because of computer glitches on an all too frequent basis.

- If inflation spirals, then using a wheelbarrow to move your money around is just impractical, but it is an approach that is used in some developing and so-called developed countries.

- You are only getting 1–3% on your savings with inflation at 2.2%, down from 4+% in 2012. This means your savings will stagnate the longer they stay in the bank, even with rate rises. Why? Because a rise in the Bank of England Base Rate moves quickly to increase the cost of a mortgage and other loan borrowing, but moves much more slowly to increase the rate savers receive!

How to choose

How can you tell which investments make sense? What are the pros and cons of the stock market and other investment classes? ROI or cash-on-cash return gives you a tangible equation to compare different investments based on the net return (or profit) that you get on an annual basis for each sum invested.

The ROI formula is simple:

- Above the dividing line is the net profit from the investment. So, in the example of buying a buy-to-let property, above the line is the annual net rent. This is the gross rent from the tenant minus the letting agent fees, the mortgage and the property insurance. This could also be the interest earned on savings or other forms of investment income.

- Below the dividing line is all the cash costs that are needed to get the property to a point where it produces rent. Therefore, there is the deposit on the property; the solicitor, surveyor and broker fees; the costs to refurbish the property; gas certificates, tenant search fees; and, when you are sourcing for a bespoke client, my sourcing fee. There could also be the cost of investing cash into another form of investment deal.

When you divide the smaller top number by the larger bottom number, you will get a figure of less than one – maybe 0.10 or anything from 0.04–0.35. This is effectively a percentage (10, 4 or 35%) and it means this investment would earn you that percentage of income, and so you can compare it to the potentially less risky investment offered by savings accounts and the rate of interest you could earn from the bank or building society.

You can use this information to calculate potential profit shares in a business or investments in anything from shares, gold or property. This is a comparable measure that enables you to calculate the difference between two investment opportunities. It includes all the costs involved, rather than the yield which some investors use – especially in the property world – as this is a broad, gross figure.

I hope you can now see that you not only need to change the way you think about property, you also need to question how to get the best return on your savings.

LESSON 5: BUILD A PROPERTY PORTFOLIO NOW

You now understand leverage and how to apply that to your resources. You also know what it means to understand the return on your time that's been invested. This is the cornerstone to understanding how and where can you grow your money.

I have also briefly hinted that you can spend, save or invest and that there are different asset classes when you invest. Assets are financial products that you can invest in, each with different characteristics that give you different levels of control over them. Let's look at the asset classes in slightly more detail and then I will explain ROI, or return on investment (cash invested), and how you can use it as a way to compare how efficiently you are using your money.

There are five broad asset classes:

- Commodities
- Stocks and shares or fixed interest bonds
- Business and property
- Precious metals, crypto or cash

Commodities are the products of businesses that can be traded. These include electricity, oil and other fuels, food and drink, such as wine, coffee and corn, as well as minerals and metals. You effectively buy a share of a product, mostly bought through a broker, and gamble it. As this is traded around the world on the commodities market, demand for the primary or raw product rises and so does your profit.

Stocks and shares in their simplest form are where you give some money in exchange for a percentage of the future profit of a company you like. You can't influence any of the decisions the company makes about its business practices, as you are a passive observer of the performance. Alternatively, you can invest in fixed interest stocks to mitigate the risk of stock market fluctuations.

Business is straightforward. You can invest your money in your own business. You can invite others to join you, and you can share the profit when you make it. If this is your own business, then you will have control over the decisions and the profits, but you will need to invest your time alongside your money to see the best returns.

Precious metals are relatively simple to understand. Here, you exchange your cash for an equivalent value of a precious metal – gold and silver are typical. The price of the metal may change by the time you wish to exchange it back into currency, but it is considered a more stable investment. I see crypto-currencies in this class too. You invest at a certain price which may go up or down. Cash or savings also experience the same fluctuations in real terms if you factor in interest rates and inflation. I don't see these forms of investment as much better than stocks and shares, in that you have no control over their value.

Property is something that you can buy, enhance, control and use. Above all, you can ask to raise a loan against its value and increase the return you get from it. Again, we come back to the point about a relatively small island with high demand for land. I'll use an example of property to show you both leverage in a simple form and how income is generated.

If you can imagine having £200,000 in cash (or released as equity from your home), you have a few choices:

You might be able to buy one house outright, outside of London, for that amount and live in it. You would get no rental income as you are the tenant so your wages would pay for the mortgage. What if you bought the house outright and placed a tenant in the property to pay the rent? Because you have no mortgage all the rental income would be profit.

If your tenants stay all year at £850 permonth, that would be £10,200 per year.

What if you took your £200,000 and used a mortgage to leverage it so that you used only £50,000 as a deposit for each of four houses worth £200,000 each. Now you have to pay a mortgage of £150,000 at 3.5%, for example. That would take £5,250 per year out of your profit of £10,200, leaving a profit of £4,950 on each house. That's a grand total of £19,800 for all four properties. Is that worth considering? In real life, you would have other buying costs, such as a solicitor, surveyor and broker fees.

Could we do better? What if, instead of buying near London, we went further north where property prices are cheaper? What if average house prices were £100,000 to make the maths easier? In fact, I have bought property at £51,000 for two-bedroomed houses and I regularly buy at £95,000-115,000.

I will be even more accurate now and say that each property requires £50,000 cash to cover the deposit on the property and all the costs of buying from fees and surveys to repairs and finding a tenant. Using a mortgage to leverage your money, you could buy up to 4 properties with the same like-for-like 25% mortgage deposit. The total rent from a three-bedroom house is about £7,200 per annum and the cost of the mortgage about £2,625.

This would mean that each little house would give you £7,200 minus £2,625 mortgage costs = £4,575 profit per house. Multiple that by 4 houses = £18,300 per year profit compared to £7,200 for one house bought outright without a mortgage.

You can see the power of leverage in this example. In real life, the profits are lower by approximately 15-20%, because you need to allow for void periods and repairs. The rates of return in London is 3-7% compared to the North of England which offers a 10–12% return. That is the power of leverage.

The question becomes this – once you have decided on the life you want and you understand the resources you have, how can you make the most of them by using leverage and outsourcing? The previous example is raw and illustrative, but I hope it makes the point.

As material possessions become less important and a house does not necessarily have to be a home, the shift will be fascinating to watch as it is bound to involve the clash of intergenerational values. Not just arguments in families, but politicians will be out of kilter and businesses will struggle to keep up.

Do you understand how your potential property investment model or strategy could give you the flexibility you want now and financial security for the future? It will be possible to work in partnership as a family to create this if you start to think about property differently – NOW!

Imagine if you invested in property today at relatively low prices. That property would provide income to support the family as a whole until certain demands arose like school fees, university fees, business start-up costs, elderly parents or early retirement.

The main portfolio would remain as the core asset, secured in a limited company to protect the assets and income and all spending would come from the revenue the rental income generated. In approximately 10 years, the value of the portfolio would double – so you might make a decision to adapt your strategy.

To really understand how property could help you to create a revolutionary Non-Traditional Retirement Plan to fund the next 40 years or more of your life, read my new book *The Wealthy Retirement Plan: A revolutionary guide to living the rest of your life in style* published in January 2019, or check out our *Readiness to Retire Wealth Scorecard* on our website.

You could sell one of the 4 properties in the portfolio and use the capital that is released from the one house sale of approximately £200,000 to pay most of the outstanding mortgages. Your portfolio will still consist of four mortgages of £75,000 each, equalling £300,000. This would give you, from our early example, three properties with only £100,000 in outstanding mortgage debt across the entire portfolio.

You might be worried that your income will reduce if you sell some of your portfolio; however, if you use the capital to clear the mortgages, then you would own 2 mortgage-free properties which would mean 100% of the rental income is yours, minus the maintenance costs, of course.

You would have an ongoing cashflow of approximately £14,400 from two mortgage-free properties and a further £4,575 from the remaining mortgaged property if all the other factors stayed the same, including interest rates. This is £18,975 per annum, which would be £675.00 a year more than when all the properties were mortgaged.

You might be wondering about the original £200,000. If that was released from your home with a mortgage, how has that been paid? You could use the £183,000 cashflow you have had over the last ten years. You could use the cashflow to add to the portfolio and buy more property and then clear everything at the end. It all depends on what you need to earn from property, what resources you have to start with and, of course, your approach to risk, leverage and property management. It also depends on the life you want to create for yourself and your attitude towards opportunity and risk.

This is just an example. It is designed to get you thinking about property in a different way, one that suits the demand of future generations. And yes – for the detailed people – I made the property value double and did not double the rent. What if, once all the numbers became precise, you only earned £100,000 in 10 years for just making a decision today, or only had £10,000 extra per year for working no more than one day a month?

That's why I spend my time and money investing in property and why I help my clients invest in property. That is how you can have a lifestyle of choice and ongoing financial security. That is why I write books about investing in property. I hope that by sharing my experience and understanding, you will be able to make more informed decisions for you, your family and your financial future.

If you want to know how this will work for you personally, get in touch and we can arrange a resource audit and personal investment strategy session.

LESSON 6: WHO IS PART OF YOUR TEAM?

Group work at school or university was always a nightmare of mismatched personalities, as it meant that different work ethics were bound together and we were all reliant on one another to get a good grade.

With a more fluid and less visible workforce, many of which work online or in different countries, personalities are less important than the quality of the work produced and the adherence to deadlines and profit targets. These are the classic markers used by online work environments, like PeoplePerHour, Fiverr. com or other freelance online marketplaces.

In the past, businesses have struggled to grow as increased sales mean that a larger staff team is needed. Employment legislation, tax and the other costs of an employee were a huge commitment and prohibitive – but now businesses often employ some-one for a project and that is it. When the project is over the team member leaves. This means a business can grow opportunistically and adapt more easily to a volatile economic environment. Long-term sustain-able growth can then evolve out of these increased profits, leading to large full-time teams and a dynamic business culture that meets the needs of loyal custom-ers.

If you are already busy in your own business or job, then the ability to take on flexible and part-time staff means you can leverage other people's time and grow your wealth. I have a financial director, a book-keeper, a personal assistant, a social media expert, a publisher, an editor and a marketing and PR expert who are all part of my team. They work a set number of hours or as part of a contract. They are not 'mine' exclusively, but they work to agreed deadlines and generate or save my income. We have all worked together for over ten years, even the newest member has been with us for three years. This has created the best of both worlds – a flexible team that under-stands what we are all focused on achieving. They understand and buy into our company values of transparency and trust.

Have you identified your team? Who do you need to help you find, fix and fill a portfolio of cash-generating properties? Where in the country should you start? What property types should you look for? Who do you need on your team? Do you have the knowledge and understanding to make those decisions or do you need help with that too?

Do you know what you need to know?

This is the biggest question of all – who are you learning from? What are you learning? Is it relevant to the life that you want to have and the world you are entering? Or is it from dusty tomes taught by people in the shadows rather than on the cutting edge of business?

Financial education is what matters. Understanding how leverage works, as I showed you in the examples earlier (page 127) matters. Understanding what ROI means and how you can compare the ROI for any decision you make matters. Understanding what your time is worth and what money is worth as a relative source of exchange matters.

Remember that time is also something that can be leveraged along with cash and, of course, knowledge. In Chapter 5, I will explore case studies to help you envisage the different paths you can take to create a property portfolio.

I will make one caveat, I do not know you or your personal circumstances. This is not financial advice. I am sharing my experience, knowledge and understanding in order to help you challenge traditional thinking and develop your own goals, which will give you and your family the sort of financial security and lifestyle you want.

LESSON 7: LETTING GO OF OLD HABITS

This will probably be easier for your children than for you or your parents. Have you realised the cold hard truth yet that we, as a society, are bankrupt? Can you admit that you need to provide for your own future? Your lifestyle, as stressful as it has been in the past, will mean that you will live longer. You have seen your parents and grandparents start to struggle as they have to cut back to conserve a cash reserve for when they get older. What sort of life and retirement do you want? What life do you want for your children and your grandchildren?

So now do you accept that it is time to invest in cashflowing property assets?

While you enjoy your share of technical gadgets, you also need to recognise the difference between good debt, which is money borrowed to buy income-generating assets, and bad debt, which is money borrowed or personal capital spent on material luxuries that incur high-interest rates, as you cannot afford to clear the loans or credit cards. You will know for certain that your next car will be funded by profit made from your tenants.

This means your path to a wealthier life is exponentially faster than your parents or peers, who are still trapped selling their time for money, which never seems to be enough. It's a good job you are growing your wealth because you can see friends around you who are starting to run out of money and they will need you to help them – to show them what you have learnt before it's too late.

The best thing you did was read *Property for the Next Generation*. By releasing money from your house, you were able to work with me and my team to start investing in property much sooner than your peers. Your healthy portfolio has provided the cashflow and feeling of security that will enable you to make better decisions. Now you can focus on helping others.

❙ SUMMARY AND QUESTIONS

If you would like to create your own personal investment strategy, then follow the lessons in this book:

SUMMARY

➡ Review your personal financial position – think about what you are spending your money on and ask yourself if you could use it to build your financial security more easily if you leveraged it.

➡ Consider your actual asset, cash reserves and even equity in your own home. What rate of interest are you earning from your current financial strategies, and could you be earning more?

➡ Think about your time. Do you have time, or knowledge, to identify cashflowing property, often outside of the capital and large cities?

➡ Who can help you to clarify and then achieve your goals?

There are resources and an online course to help you in the training section of my website (www.VickiWusche.com) and there is more information at the back of the book about how I can help.

QUESTIONS

1. What do you want? What do you value? What do you enjoy? Make a list.

2. Are you ready to take responsibility for the future you want? Complete a budget and work out what it will cost and how much you will need to earn.

3. Think about how you spend your time and what it's worth. Could you spend it more wisely?

4. Ask yourself if you need to spend money on the luxuries now, or if you could wait for your tenants to buy them for you?

5. Do you understand how business is changing and can you adapt to make the most of this opportunity?

6. Who do you need on your team? Who do you need to talk to or meet with?

7. Do you have an outline of a property investment strategy?

CHAPTER

4

WHAT DO YOU WANT IN YOUR LIFE AND HOW MUCH WILL IT COST?

Whether or not we consciously recognise it, we all want our lives to be like something. Our decisions have been influenced by the values and culture of our parents, peers and teachers. In a sense, we are bound by the reality of those around us, but is their reality relevant anymore?

If you could start without any kind of limitations or generational beliefs, what sort of life would you want? A good place to start is to think about what is important to you. What do you value? Having said this, a lot of your beliefs will still have been influenced by your parents.

So start a list. Think about what really matters to you in your life and, in turn, about the way you earn a living. Is variety important? What about stability and structure? Is status important or knowing you have done something that made a difference? We are all different and there is no need for judgement to be laid on these choices. It is just a 'conversation' about how you think you want to live the next 30–40 years of your adult life. For some, having a job and being part of a team or an organisation is comforting, satisfying and fulfilling; while the idea of working alone and motivating yourself every day seems unnecessarily unpleasant. Any choice you make does not mean that you will be forced to give up your job. In fact, being employed will make future funding so much easier.

Other people think that work means constraint, routine and rules – that's another opinion. It also might mean responsibility, commitment, achievement and self-motivation. Know what you want to get out of life and what you value. These intrinsic values shape the choices you make.

Another area to consider is your lifestyle needs. Again, there are no judgements. Do you want to travel, grow your family, work in a city or 'make things'? Does technology excite you? Would you like to work and live with lots of people, or do you prefer numbers or a quieter life? What about sports, hobbies, social life, music, gadgets, cars and possessions, or are you more of a wandering spirit who prefers not to be burdened by possessions? You may love your current job and want to keep it no matter how much you earn, or you may have always wanted to open an art gallery, cake shop or even offer cruises on your own boat.

The answers to the above questions serve only to outline the potential cost of maintaining your desired lifestyle. Costs and plans that you will adapt over time as relationships change along with the world around you. To start with, if your lifestyle is more complex with more material or expensive desires, then your way of making money will need to work towards that. However, if your lifestyle is simpler – more uncluttered with a few bits of technology to support you – then you will have a different budget.

Ultimately, the message of this book is that you need to take responsibility for the life and lifestyle you want to have. You need to prepare your children for a future that is less economically certain than the past and, more importantly, a future that is not financially backed by a government with limitless pockets. You need to help your children prepare for a more mobile, technological and fast-paced world.

So now the task is to identify your resources and notice how you are currently allocating them. Are your resources working for you or someone else? Really, this is just a question of mindset. Let's think about the resources in broad terms: money, time, health, and emotional energy.

MONEY – YOU CAN SPEND, SAVE OR INVEST

The question here is about the value versus the worth of the money. Money has a value on its 'face' – it is called one pound or five pounds. Imagine a hot day. Perhaps you are in a park and a passing salesman offers you a bottle of water for a pound. Is it worth it? Yes. What if he charged £4? Would it still be worth it? It depends how hot and thirsty you are. On a hot day that water might be worth four times the cost on a colder day. The face value stays the same but it's worth to you changes.

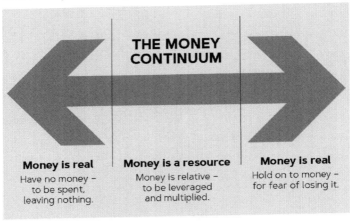

THE MONEY CONTINUUM

Money is real	**Money is a resource**	**Money is real**
Have no money – to be spent, leaving nothing.	Money is relative – to be leveraged and multiplied.	Hold on to money – for fear of losing it.

What are your thoughts about money?

When people see money as real, they want to hold on to it. For some, the more they grab, the less they have. And for others, the more they save, the less its worth because of the decisions they make.

This is where having the right sort of financial education is crucial. Think about the very rich. What do they own a lot of? The answer is property and land. This is because we are an island with a finite supply; therefore, it will always be of value and/or worth to someone.

What has happened to pensioners over recent years, since the start of the latest recession in 2007–2008? Their pensions and savings, based on stocks and shares, first shot up and then were slashed as share prices fell! What if they had just held on to the cash in a pot by their bed? Then it would have lost between 4–5% of its value in real terms each year because prices rose due to inflation, but their money stayed the same.

What if they had put the money in the bank? Well, they might have been getting 1–2% interest, maybe 3% if they were lucky, but they were still losing out overall against inflation.

They could have invested in property. If they had bought before the crash, then their property's worth compared to someone else's might have fallen, but a property's value lies in the rental income it generates. As long as they have a tenant, then their property is still worth the same to them!

If you consider money as an exchange mechanism – something to be exchanged – then you will start to see that you can put it to work for you. This is what I will explain, in greater detail, in Chapter 5.

The biggest problem with money is that once you have spent it – it is gone – it leaves your hands and passes to another person. Most often, it is exchanged for something that you valued at the time.

Look at the example of buying a coffee from a coffee shop on page 121. The example shows that if you spend your money on a latte every day for 21 days, you would have spent £57.75, but you would have lost the opportunity to make millions. Surely, you'll never buy another coffee again.

In the title of this chapter, I ask the question: how much will it cost? i.e. this lifestyle of yours. This is relatively easy to budget. You just take all the expenses in your life and the projected expenses of any business or immediate additional outlay and complete an income and expenses budget. Tracking your money on a monthly basis is a brilliant way to maintain focus.

The real answer to the question, 'how much will it cost?' depends on whether you are spending money you have to earn or whether you are spending money that has been made to work for you and is time-free cash.

So, here is a final set of questions:

- Can you now see that you can invest your financial resources in such a way that money could be seen as your 'employee', i.e. its sole job is to earn you money? You would have control over the decisions and results that surround its use and would have the ability to influence how much it earned.

- Do you now see that money is not real but has, in effect, a relative value based on how it is used? There is a decision to make about whether your money should continue to be spent in the short term, on material objects, for example, or invested in order to earn cashflow, which could then be used to buy things while maintaining the size of the capital sum.

You have now a clear idea about the type of lifestyle you want and have costed this out on a spreadsheet. You are starting to get curious about money, including what is it worth compared to its face value and how can you make it work for you? You have also started to question whether money is real or relative, especially as you understand that it is most likely to be based on debt anyway! Now you need to think about how you want to spend your time as this is another of your valuable assets.

TIME – YOU CAN SPEND IT, SAVE IT OR INVEST IT

Once you are in control of your money, then the next resource to think about is your time. Once the burden of exchanging your time for money is removed and replaced with the constant flow of cash from assets bought with your goals in mind, then your whole way of thinking changes. You can actually start to revisit those long-forgotten goals of travel, business, hobbies or childhood dreams.

Time is like money in that we give it a unitary value of hours and minutes. However, does the hour you spent on the train with lots of hot commuters have the same value as it would for a soldier returning from duty abroad who is seeing their son or daughter for the first time in six months?

Time is worse than money in that we, as individuals, only have a finite amount. You can always borrow money from someone else, but when you borrow an hour you don't really get it – you just give what you were going to do to someone else. This is why you need to think carefully about the value of your time and how you spend it. Do you spend your time doing a job that you love, either working for yourself or for someone else or doing a job you hate?

The great thing about the internet is that it speeds things up, giving you information at your fingertips. You can work from home and save commuting. You can do online banking, online shopping and save the time you would normally spend queueing and travelling. But what are you doing with the time you save? Add these ideas to your list of things that are important to you and you enjoy.

HEALTH AND EMOTIONAL ENERGY – THE FOUNDATION OF YOUR SUCCESS

Without good health or emotional resilience, you will struggle. These are more important than both money and time combined. A doctor can make you better, but only you can make yourself sick. The stress you bring into your life and the food that you eat all contribute to the levels of hormones and chemicals in your body. How are you spending your energy and resilience, because that's what we are actually talking about?

A quick word on emotional resilience here, because that is something you will need in bucket loads if you decide that either property investment or working for yourself is your path. Resilience is vital if you are to overcome challenges, to work every day when you need to, to make tough calls and hard decisions and – for some people – to make a sales call or do the accounts! Even more important is the resilience to ignore all those comments by doomsayers who are not educated like you, but rely on the old teachings of school and the daily papers.

So now you can see your life in terms of the resources that you can spend or invest. The next question is: can you let go of old habits…?

CHAPTER

5

TEACH YOUR 22-YEAR-OLD TO BUY THEIR OWN HOUSE

In Chapter 2, I explained how everything that we thought was true and real is actually shifting under our feet. The government cannot fulfil the promises made by the generations of years gone by.

More than a dozen prime ministers have failed to respond sufficiently to the fact that the accounting books just don't balance, and that we, as a country, and now it seems as a world, are spending so much more than we can ever possibly hope to repay. We are, in fact, spiralling into debt at an alarming and compounding rate. If our country was a family and the government its parents, then you'd hope that one of the adults would notice what was wrong and do something about it!

In post-war Britain, we shared different values and beliefs. These were born out of the fact that life was tough. The population was not reliant on handouts from the government yet and the demands on our health service were not as great as they are now. They did not have the burgeoning obesity crisis we do, or as many of the various cancers, dementia and other extreme diseases of old age. ME (or 'yuppie flu') and attention deficit disorders had not been recognised yet. Back then, it was impossible to cure many illnesses with a simple pill or 'keyhole' surgical procedure that can now extend the lives of thousands of people.

Today, there is pressure from league tables to put every child through free education, regardless of their capability or future aspirations, until they are eighteen years old. There is also the added pressure of an increasingly ageing population that is reliant on the government to support them for 20, 30 or even 40 years after retirement. This level of social support system cannot continue; it can't afford to.

In Chapter 3, I systematically described the seven lessons they will not be teaching your child in school. I explained how money is really debt and, therefore, if you don't keep it moving, it actually loses value as the rate of inflation erodes your asset and equity.

In Chapter 4, I explained how we should think about money differently and see it as a tool that we can master and make work for us.

Money can either cost you a fortune (literally if you don't manage the accumulating debt) or enable you to live a comfortable life that is free from worry or stress.

Learning to spend from earned recurring residual income rather than capital will mean that you have your own personal cash generating machine for generations to come. Use credit cards and fail to manage the interest costs and you will end up working for the banks for the rest of your life in order to clear your debt.

In this chapter, I will explain different strategies that you can use to create your family portfolio, from buying a single investment property to teaching your child to buy a property portfolio that will enable them to have lifelong financial freedom.

I will show you a model, where you can take advantage of the property market, get in at the 'bottom' and watch as the increasing value of your portfolio effectively erodes your debt while also generating cash to pay school fees, university fees or give you flexibility and security, especially if your children are under 16 or 17 years old. The bottom of the market is always now, compared to waiting until your children are 18 years old or older, as prices by then will have risen even higher.

CASE STUDY 1
Save up and buy it yourself

As with anything I do (either with clients or for myself) I need to know 'why?' I don't see this as an emotional process. So many people buy 'homes' based on love or some other emotion. This is a brilliant investment. Having said that, I recognise that buying a property for the first time may be exciting, scary and even confusing. My aim is to approach the property as a business investment that you may or may not live in, now or in the future – an investment that you will not sell, but will grow in value and generate enough income to pay for itself.

This is the story of how my daughter, Kimberley, set her mind to buy her first property at the age of 22 years old. Before I start the story in detail, I think it is important to say that this model worked because I encouraged her to go through the thinking process that's outlined in Chapter 4 on page 149. She had decided what she wanted in her life and what resources she had access to – including checking with me about possible financial handouts (and it was fair that she asked – it is what young people have been taught to do). She then identified her resource gap and set about dealing with it. It was successful because it was driven by her and not by me.

So why does your child want to buy a property? It's crucial that they can answer this question. It might be a simple answer, such as 'I want to leave home'. In an ideal world, your children might like to live near work or university, but it is important to check afford-ability. I will explain the reason for this later.

Asking 'Why?' speaks to the motivation for the purchase and some young people have spent the last three years or more reading in the press that they can't afford to invest, as I mentioned while discussing Myth 6 in Chapter 2 on page 88. All the while, television programmes, such as *Homes Under the Hammer* and presenters like Martin Roberts and Sarah Beeny, demonstrate how you can buy property cheaply and then turn it around and sell it for a massive profit. That is why I asked about the underlying motivation.

If the desire is to follow the television pro-grammes and invest in order to gain a capital return and get a lump sum on the sale of the property, then this is never an easy or straight forward strategy to follow. Editors organise events to create a good TV show, the property market does what it wants when it wants. Explaining about income-generating assets and spending from revenue rather than capital, as well as all the figures from Chapter 1 that relate to future rising house prices, should show that other strategies make better long-term sense. It will also show young people how it is the first step to building their long-term property portfolio.

Let's move past the motivation for a minute and start to look at what they want to buy. Now, in some parts of the country house prices might be dictating your choices, or rather be limiting them. It's important to look at a few house types through the eyes of a professional investor and consider their functionality, suitability and value for money.

STEP 1 – CREATING AND MANAGING A CREDIT SCORE

As discussed in Chapter 3, Lesson 1 on page 111, lenders use credit scores as a way of calculating how likely a person is to pay or default on a loan. My daughter and I addressed this immediately. Kimberley was open to ideas and instruction because a good credit score is so important and yet so easy to ruin.

All of Kimberley's credit cards were already on direct debits, as we had previously discussed finance. So now we obtained copies of her credit scores and credit reports from the main agencies. Her scores were high and clean, so no repair work was needed. If you find that credit scores for members of your family home are damaged and poor, it can reflect on the entire family.

▌ STEP 2 – AFFORDABILITY

Next, we spoke about the location and property type in a general way in order to get a sense of the goal and whether or not it was realistic. I understood that maximum mortgage loans are calculated on a multiple of the family income – so that three, four or five times a salary can be loaned. These figures can be based on a joint wage, as well as a single income.

I gave Kimberley a rough maximum purchase price that was based on her salary. So, for example, if someone earned £25,000 per annum and the multiplier was four times their salary, then they could borrow a maximum of £100,000. Now that is the maximum loan and could represent 95% or even 90% of the purchase price – let's take 90%.

So £100,000 (potential maximum loan) divided by 90 (the loan to value ratio of the mortgage) x 100 (to help calculate the actual property asking price) = approximately £111,111.

This means a young person earning £25,000 per annum, could view properties that were for sale between £111,000–125,000 with a view to agreeing on a maximum purchase price of £111,111, knowing that a lender would lend 90% of the purchase price (i.e. £99,999) and that their salary would meet the affordability conditions of the loan.

STEP 3 – CAN YOU AFFORD TO LIVE IN YOUR NEW HOUSE

I honestly think that working through catalogues and online stores to plan and cost everything needed for Kimberley's home was a reward after completing the income and expenses sheet. She became an expert at finding deals and gradually buying items as they came on sale over the two years it took her to start looking for and then buy her first home.

By the time she had her purchase offer accepted, Kimberley already had a chest full of all the minor household items and so only needed to order white goods, a sofa and a bed.

STEP 4 – MAKING THE RIGHT MOVE

By using online search sites, such as Rightmove.co.uk or Zoopla.co.uk, you can search for property that your child could theoretically afford to buy. By entering a postcode or town, choosing the property type – one, two or three bedroomed – and setting a maximum value of £125,000, the search engine returned a list of properties that matched our criteria. If this does not work in the precise location you want to live, extend the search radius from a quarter of a mile to one mile, and so on.

Understandably, this will cover a massive area of properties in London so keep searching until you find the appropriate area based on pricing. Move your centre point to the town to your left or your right and start again. It can take some time to refine the searching process, but possible postcodes and affordable areas will start to emerge in the end.

The next stage is to think about the consequences of that area and how it will affect travelling to work and travelling to see friends, family and your social life. Ultimately, everyone wants a home that is convenient for all aspects of their lives. Parents and married couples will consider the impact of local schools, for instance.

▍ STEP 5 – FINANCIAL INTELLIGENCE

Alongside the task of checking credit scores and learning about online searching, we discussed savings and other financial assets. Kimberley completed our income and expenses budget. This gave us a clear picture of her cashflow. We calculated what was true while she lived at home and worked out what would change when she left home. For example:

- Rent or housekeeping would become mortgage payments
- She would have utility bills, council tax and household insurance to pay
- Food costs would be joined by cleaning products and toiletries

■ She would need the funds to furnish the property, not just large items, such as a cooker or fridge, but everything from corkscrews and potato peelers to plates and sheets

STEP 6 – PROPERTY TYPES

It is important to understand property as an investment (even though, if bought as a home, it will be a liability). There are cost implications to property types.

Flats

The challenge with flats is both structural and financial. Looking at the structural issues, every property in the block is likely to be broadly the same. This makes differentiation more difficult when it comes to either selling or renting it out for an income that you want.

You cannot easily change the windows, as there may be rules imposed by the managing agent or the freeholder, or change the front door, and you certainly cannot add an extension. This means opportunities to add value through structural change are almost zero. And those that do exist will be limited and require freeholder permission.

If your property is part of a block, there will also be overheads for managing the property, such as keeping communal areas clean, lit and maintained, as well as costs, such as management and accounting.

This is where the financial challenge occurs because there will be limitations to your power to influence the repairs or repair costs as everyone involved with the block will have to agree.

Houses

Now consider a house. Even on a street of similar properties, you – as the freeholder – can change the doors and windows or add an extension to the roof or rear (subject to local council approval). You are in charge of the maintenance and upkeep without the need for management costs.

New-build houses

A new-build house, compared to an older property, can certainly prove a buying challenge for young people, especially if, as parents, you have been inclined to repeatedly buy older properties and do them up to sell and start the process again. New-build properties will most likely offset a greater level of comfort and 'ready-to-move-in' marketing against actual floor space. Older properties, even 1960s ex-council properties, will appear significantly larger than their equivalent new-build house. Floor space and the height of the ceilings can give a much larger feel to a room.

The second challenge comes from the same problem as we see in flats – differentiation. If the new-build property is on a new estate, then making it stand out from a neighbour's property may be difficult. The other devil in the detail of new-build properties is their 'ready-made' nature. The purchase price includes the carpeting and the cost of the fridge. When you borrow your loan to buy the bricks and mortar, you are also paying 3–5% for 20+ years on the cost of a fridge.

After 25 years, a fridge that would have cost £250 could have almost doubled in cost, as a result of mortgage interest rates over the last 25 years, instead of just the two or three years offered by Curry's, Argos or even AO.com!

Of course, buying an older house can be challenging, especially if it requires both renovation work and updating. However, it may simply be a case of redecoration, which all helps in the process of adding value.

So, the process included:

1. Creating and managing a credit score.

2. Affordability – Calculate what you can afford to buy based on what you can afford to borrow. As well as using the affordability calculator, actually think about the impact on your personal income and expenses in real life.

3. Can you afford to live in your new house? Budget and plan for household goods while you are saving for your deposit.

4. Making the right move – Define your target area. Where can you reasonably afford to live and does that make sense?

5. Financial Intelligence – Calculate your income and expenses and make adjustments in order to save the 5–10% deposit that's required. If you already live at home and are determined, then this is very achievable with two years of hard saving, thinking about expenses and shifting all birthday and Christmas presents towards your goal of owning your own home. If it isn't, work together as a family to make this a reality.

6. Property types – Think about what makes sense and suits your needs. You might think a flat is a good place to start, but it is important to consider the cost implications.

Once you have mastered budgeting, affordability and the theory of house buying, you can start to take a serious look at what is possible. Have a practice run before you are ready to buy, so you can make adjustments to your plan, if needed. When you do get to the stage of viewing properties and defining your area, carry out the following simple checks:

» 1. Get to know your area

What is the area like at 8am on a weekday morning, 10pm on a Saturday evening and 11am on a Sunday morning? By visiting the area at different times, you can see the impact of school and work traffic on the surrounding roads during and out of rush hour. Are local pubs noisy and what about church bells? Check out the flood zone maps and airport flight paths!

Practise your new route to work. It is best to do so on a weekday during rush hour. So leave home early, drive to your new target home area and then on to work – this will be a really valuable lesson.

Finally, think about your habits. Do you belong to a gym? If so, where is it in relation to your new home? Are you on a course? If so, will the travelling impact on your studies? Where is your nearest shop? Are there local superstores or smaller convenience stores nearby that you could use?

» 2. The buying process

The second phase is learning about the property and the buying process – and what questions to ask. The fact that I am a professional property investor who buys property for a living was an advantage. We waited until Kimberley had saved the 10% deposit, plus enough money to buy a bed, fridge, cooker, etc. and pay for a survey and broker and solicitor fees. This came to a total of £24,000.

To achieve a savings rate of £1,000 per month, Kimberley's social life adapted. Fun activities included going for walks and buying memberships of both a cinema and gym. Friends could all then meet for free and train, swim, go for a sauna and visit the cinema for a low monthly fee. She also spent a lot of time meeting at the houses or flats of friends who had already bought property. She had a goal and was focused on achieving it.

We knew that Kimberley's target mortgage was a maximum of £180,000, which worked both in terms of affordability, according to the lender, and her own personal budget. So we knew that based on a 90% mortgage, she could buy a property for £200,000 and we could even shop a bit higher and negotiate down from the asking price.

Therefore, if you start out knowing that you want to negotiate, you need to know what situation the vendor is in:

- How long has the house been on the market? The longer the better as this means the vendor might be keener to move.

- Where are they moving to? Do they already have somewhere in mind and so are keen to move, or are they not in a rush?

- Why are they moving? It could be to meet the schooling needs of their children, due to divorce or family sickness, or it might be work-related.

Every question that was asked conversationally as we walked around the house was designed to calculate how quickly the vendor wanted to move and, therefore, how likely they would be to accept an offer on their asking price.

» 3. Viewing like a surveyor

Looking at a property in a dispassionate and non-emotional way, like a mortgage surveyor, is a vital skill. What condition is the roof in, and what about the chimney, gutters or soffits? What is the condition of the windows and general exterior? All these questions indicate the cost of immediate or future repairs.

Inside is easier, as it falls under the headings of 'general decoration' (after all, it is likely that most people will want to repaint before they move in) and 'key expense items', like the electrics, heating system and state of the bathroom and kitchen. What condition are they all in?

Most families know someone who understands a bit about building. Therefore, once a shortlist of potential properties is compiled, invite someone to come with you. If you don't want to take a relative, then ask a local builder.

After saving the amount that's needed, the lesson moves on to property management and conditioning – get help if you need it. Above all, consider the type of survey you get when you buy the property. The cheapest surveys are just valuations for the use of the lender. If you do not have access to family or friends with property expertise, then invest in a more expensive but reassuring full-structural survey.

» 4. The mechanics of buying

As a parent and homeowner, you probably know the actual mechanics of buying. I explicitly explained the process to my daughter. This included details about offering on a property and the acceptance of an offer, the questions and information the solicitor would need, the information and process of applying for a mortgage and, finally, the process of exchange and completion.

You, as a parent, will know a lot of this already, but there are three points I would like to highlight:

1. If you don't talk your children through the whole process, they will be unable to prepare themselves or ask the right questions.

2. Think like a property investor. This property will now stay in the family for a considerable amount of time. The best time to make money on a property is when you buy it for the lowest price possible. Be prepared to make your offer and, if it's not accepted, walk away. If you are not buying with an emotional 'head', then this process will be easier and you will get a better deal.

3. Above all, be polite and respectful. Unless you are buying a repossession, you will be walking

around someone's home. Whether or not the property is the right price or suits your taste, imagine the owner is in the room with you.

Explain to your children that they could continue to maximise their income and expenses and work out how much they can save towards their next property. You will not be able to rely on property price increases and remortgages, and I would counsel against the overuse of that strategy, but once you have satisfied your desire to buy a 'home', the next property can be bought with tenants in mind.

So, in summary, the 'save up and buy' model is as follows:

A. Understand personal spending and cashflow budgets.
B. Know how much you can borrow.
C. Work out where you can afford to live.
D. Research.
E. Save.
F. Look.
G. Buy.
H. Do it again.

▌ LIVING THE DREAM

I have to say that buying her first house was an act of extreme determination on Kimberley's part. She knew what she wanted, then worked out what she had to do and did it. Yes, there were times when I saw her go out two nights in a row (shock) or buy a new pair of shoes (bigger shock), but she found a way to work hard, play sensibly and get what she wanted quickly.

This is why I started with the question 'why?' Once your child knows why they want their own home or investment property they will be determined to achieve it.

CASE STUDY 2
Starting young

This is less of a case study and more a story of a family that has enabled their children to explore an adult world.

I knew one of my clients long before I helped her to invest. Her daughter was with her every event we met at. Not because the mum was a single parent who had no one to look after her daughter, but because her daughter was interested in what her mum got up to.

I have known the daughter for over sixteen years now. In the early days, she brought her colouring books, then later, a Gameboy to keep her entertained during the two or three-hour long property meeting. Between the ages of 9 and 12, she even attended three-day events and heard Robert Kiyosaki, Daniel

Priestley and Tony Robbins, amongst others, speak about money, business economics and success.

Now, the daughter is comfortable in the company of adults and is like a smaller member of the group, able to hold a confident conversation in her own right. Most importantly, she is gaining an education in finance, business and world economics like no other child in her school. I can't help but see that as an advantage; not an advantage over others, but an advantage for her in her life and her future.

Of course, on top of all this, her mum is a successful entrepreneur, who started her own business after we worked together to create her cashflowing property.

CASE STUDY 3
Follow a career path

The children of two of my clients have both taken a practical approach to learning about property investment by getting jobs in the business: one as a letting agent; the other as an estate agent.

There are many reasons why this is a brilliant apprenticeship for any young person who thinks they want to make a career out of property investment. First, because of the practical sales experience, and, secondly, because of the research and contacts that they can accumulate.

Depending on where a person actually works, they can gain experience of the property types, the client types and the types of questions and challenges that are associated with setting up a business around sourcing (finding) property deals for other investors. This is the core message behind my second book, *Make More Money from Property: From investor thinking to a business mindset.*

CASE STUDY 4
Building a portfolio for the next generation

One of my clients has a young family and his wife stays at home to look after the children. After we spoke about his situation and his plans, he made the decision to realise some of the equity in his property. I helped him to use that money to invest in a property portfolio.

The properties provide some additional income now, but more importantly, they are a legacy for his children. Maybe he was thinking ahead to the time when the children have grown up and want to attend university.

The model is very similar to the one that I used when I released equity from my parents' home (page 125), in that the rent pays the mortgages and the profit pays for the equity release. The remaining profit adds to the family income.

This model can be adapted to any amount of equity that's released for investment purposes, as long as the rental income can afford to pay for the mortgage on the buy-to-let (investment) property and the equity release mortgage while still leaving a profit.

If having some additional income right now is not important to you, but leaving a legacy for your children or developing your own pension pot is a priority, then the model still works because accrued cashflow can be reinvested into more properties on an annual basis.

CASE STUDY 5
Investing for the future

I am working with a client who has a million pounds to invest (most clients start with £100,000). We are planning a wider portfolio strategy that would see the total portfolio being a combination of smaller buy-to-let properties in, say, the northwest where we can get a 15-25% return on investment over 3-5 years. We would then combine that with some larger properties that become houses of multiple occupancy (HMOs) or developments to leverage his capital.

Minimising risk and exposure is one of the most critical parts of the strategic planning process that I support my clients to go through.

Part of the risk of investment is the ongoing ability of the new landlord to manage the portfolio once created. One complex factor is the distance of the portfolio from the investor's home and the number of new organisations the landlord needs to deal with. By grouping the investments geographically close together the landlord effectively benefits from an economy of scale, using just one letting agent, and build team.

This grouping of all the investment 'eggs into one basket' needs to then be off-set through a balance of strategies. As effectively all the cash invested would be in one area for the above stated benefits, the risk of exposure from a change in the market can then be achieved by a spread of investment strategies. Using a combination of property types, tenant types and strategies the portfolio can offer a range of investment income from houses, and even HMOs.

Minimising exposure also means limiting the number of times that you remortgage a property. I personally believe that property can provide an indefinite return of cashflow for generations to come by letting inflation effectively reduce the debt on the property as prices rise (see Chapter 3, Lesson 3 on page 129). This means that the overall loan to value of the portfolio should aim to be below 75% and then, as prices start to rise, this will reduce to 50% and less. If you keep remortgaging property every time it increases in value, you not only reduce the cashflow but also increase the risk of exposure.

With this client, we will probably end up with a portfolio like this:

- 8 buy-to-let houses costing (worst-case scenario) £480,000 to buy.

- 2 HMOs costing (worst-case scenario) £160,000 to buy. That's a total of £640,000, leaving £360,000 for either contingencies or to follow a development strategy.

- Cashflow would be as follows:

- 8 buy-to-lets giving £375 per month = £36,000 per annum.

- 2 HMOs giving £1,500 per month (more is possible but I'm being conservative here) = £36,000 per annum.

That is a combined monthly income of £6,000, and there's almost a third of the capital left to invest in developments or further rental properties. It is also a healthy 15% plus return on investment.

❚ THE FUTURE – IS UP TO YOU

These are just a few of the examples. The key point here is that you don't know what you can do until you ask the right questions. Whatever amount you start with – whether it's a single buy-to-let that costs £50,000 cash investment to get going, which helps out your family budget by another £3,000 a year, or it's releasing a million pounds and creating a family portfolio – you will be creating a plan that's based on your personal circumstances for the life you want, and that is what is important. Please consider why you are investing before you start and make sure that you discuss this with your family and your new property team.

Whether your children read property investment books or wealth and mindset books, like mine, or others mentioned in the Bibliography, it is important to help them when they show an interest. So have conversations about money with them. Explain what interest is and what it costs, make it clear what an asset and a liability is, and describe how once you have spent money from your capital it is gone, but if you invest your capital and spend the profit and the capital will keep laying the golden eggs. Help them to understand all this because we need them to get the country and the world out of this debt mess we are in.

Maybe my story will have inspired you to want to learn more, or to talk to your children and share this with them. Perhaps it might inspire you to get in touch to see how we can help you create a property portfolio for the next generation and prepare your family for a wealthy future.

Don't stop now, make a plan. Do something to secure your family's financial future in uncertain times. Prepare for your retirement. Prepare your children and grandchildren's legacy. Be a family that understands money and recognises the power that comes when you learn how to invest it so that it works for you.

Above all, follow me on social media, watch my videos on Facebook and YouTube, check out my website, there are so many free resources to continue your education and that of your children.

BIBLIOGRAPHY

▌ PUBLICATIONS

Canfield, J. et al. (2009) *Chicken Soup for the Entrepreneur's Soul: Advice and Inspiration on Fulfilling Dreams*, Health Communications.

Dass, S. (2010) *Traders, Guns and Money: Knowns and Unknowns in the Dazzling World of Derivatives*, FT/Prentice Hall.

Dixon, S. (2012) *Bank to the Future: Protect Your Future Before Governments Go Bust*, Searching Finance Ltd.

Gamble, A. (2014) *Crisis Without End?: The unravelling of western prosperity*, Palgrave

Evans, T. (2015) *New Magic for a New Era: How to live a charmed life*, Tmesis Publications Ltd, UK.

Hill, N. (1960) *Think and Grow Rich*, Highroads.

Howard, C. (2005) *Turning Passions Into Profits: Three Steps to Wealth and Power*, John Wiley & Sons.

Howard, C. (2009) *Instant Wealth Wake up Rich!: Discover The Secret of The New Entrepreneurial Mind*, John Wiley & Sons.

Kiyosaki, R. (2015) *Rich Dad Poor Dad: What the Rich Teach Their Kids About*

Money That the Poor and Middle Class Do Not! Plata Publishing

Kiyosaki, R. (2017) *Why The Rich Are Getting Richer*, Plata Publishing.

Maslow, Abraham H. (Kindle version 2011) *Hierarchy of Needs: A Theory of Human Motivation.*

Massey, M. (1979) *The People Puzzle*, Reston Publishing (A Prentice Hall Co). Maxwell, J. C. (2007), *The 21 Irrefutable Laws of Leadership: Follow Them and People Will Follow You*, Thomas Nelson.

Metcalf, F. (2003) *Buddha in your Backpack*, Ulysses Press, USA.

Morris, C. R. (2009) *Two Trillion Dollar Meltdown: Easy Money, High Rollers, and the Great Credit Crash*, PublicAffairs.

Olson, J. (2005) *The Slight Edge: Turning Simple Disciplines into Massive Success*, Momentum Media.

Priestley, D. (2013) *Entrepreneur Revolution: How to develop your entrepreneurial mindset and start a business that works*, Capstone.

Rajan, R. G. (2011) *Fault Lines: How Hidden Fractures Still Threaten the World*

Economy, Princeton University Press. Redfield, J. (1994) The Celestine Prophecy, Bantam.

Rohn, J. (1993) *The Art of Exceptional Living* [Audiobook], Nightingale Conant.

Redfield, J. (1994) *The Celestine Prophecy* [Now only available as a Kindle or second hand]

Wusche, V. (2016) *Using Other People's Money: How to invest in property*, SRA Books.

Wusche, V. (2017) *Make More Money from Property: From investor thinking to a business mindset*, SRA Books

WEBLINKS:

WWW.VICKIWUSCHE.COM

PROGRAMMES, PRODUCTS AND SERVICES

I believe it is my purpose in life to share knowledge and, in doing so, inspire and educate people so that they can identify and leverage their previously untapped personal resources. Together, we will create generations of financially secure business owners and property investors and turn our economy back from the recession.

I have the writing bug, and I will continue to create a variety of books, blogs, products, services and events.

If you want to learn more about investing in property or find resources to share with your children, then please check out my other books on Amazon. We also have an online course (complete with resources) that you can access through our website called *How to Become a Successful Property Investor*.

Also on our website, you will find details of our webinars and events – some are free resources, other events are charged for – you will know what is right for you and your family.

Our latest resource is the new Readiness to Retire Wealthy Scorecard.

Free on our website – take the test. Will you be shocked or pleasantly surprised?

The scores against each of the five principles for a wealthy Non-Traditional Retirement will help you benchmark where you are on your journey. Then the personalised report will give you specific tips and ideas as to how you can move forward to living the rest of your life in style.

VICKI WUSCHE

Since 1994, Vicki has shared her knowledge and understanding of wealth, personal development and all things entrepreneurial. She has either trained or spoken in front of thousands of people across the UK. In 2013, Vicki was recognised by *The Telegraph* as one of the UK's top 25 most influential people in property.

During her time working with the government to influence education policy and teaching across London, Vicki was privileged to inspire and educate entrepreneurs at the cutting edge of a new media revolution to build better businesses. At the same time, Vicki has supported some of the most deprived people in London through her work as the director for two charitable organisations that were focused on regeneration, housing, refugees, employment and reinspiring young people.

Throughout her time working in education, and more recently in property investment and wealth creation, Vicki has constantly studied – both formally and informally – the great minds, concepts and strategies vital to business success. This has led to a Master's degree, a Diploma in Higher Education and a Master NLP qualification to mention but a few.

In September 2010, Vicki published her first book, *Using Other People's Money: How to Invest in Property*. Now in its fourth edition, it is one of five books. In March 2012, she was celebrating the launch of *Make More Money from Property: From Investor Thinking to a Business Mindset*, her eagerly awaited second book, re-released in 2017 as a second edition. Of course, this book was first published in 2012 and now joins the book portfolio in its second edition.

Throughout her employment and entrepreneurial endeavours, the driving forces behind Vicki are her family and her desire to help others maximise the resources they have – be they mental, emotional, financial or physical.

Combining all her skills and experience with an ability to passionately translate complex concepts into everyday practicalities, Vicki is focused on building property portfolios for clients who have access to financial resources. Vicki's clients recognise that this is a once-in-a-generation opportunity to build long-lasting financial security for their families and to secure and leverage their hard-earned wages before inflation erodes them. The clients, however, simply lack the time to take advantage – that's where Vicki's experience and service come into play.

Together with her business partners, Vicki offers a range of support for those looking to build their own business in property or expand their commercial businesses.

Let us help you take that next step towards financial security, and take responsibility for your family in these uncertain times.

- You can book a free 15 minute call with Vicki by using **www.VickiWusche/Appointy.com** or emailing the office through **Kimberley@Wusche-Associates.co.uk**

- Use our Readiness to Retire Wealthy Scorecard to benchmark where you are in your journey **www.VickiWusche.com/scorecard**

- And to find out more about Vicki's latest book *The Wealthy Retirement Plan; A revolutionary guide to living the rest of your life in style* - follow this link **www.VickiWusche.com/book**

Thank you

Printed in Great Britain
by Amazon